OPPOSING
VIEWPOINTS®
SERIES

America's
Global Influence

Other Books of Related Interest:

Opposing Viewpoints Series

Afghanistan

America in the Twenty-First Century

China

Democracy

Iran

National Security

Oil

Current Controversies Series

Globalization

Weapons of Mass Destruction

At Issue Series

Can Democracy Succeed in the Middle East?

Is Iran a Threat to Global Security?

"Congress shall make no law . . . abridging the freedom of speech, or of the press."

First Amendment to the U.S. Constitution

The basic foundation of our democracy is the First Amendment guarantee of freedom of expression. The Opposing Viewpoints Series is dedicated to the concept of this basic freedom and the idea that it is more important to practice it than to enshrine it.

OPPOSING VIEWPOINTS® SERIES

America's Global Influence

David M. Haugen and Susan Musser, Book Editors

GREENHAVEN PRESS

An imprint of Thomson Gale, a part of The Thomson Corporation

THOMSON

™

GALE

Detroit • New York • San Francisco • New Haven, Conn. • Waterville, Maine • London

THOMSON
GALE
™

Christine Nasso, *Publisher*
Elizabeth Des Chenes, *Managing Editor*

© 2007 Thomson Gale, a part of The Thomson Corporation.

Thomson and Star logo are trademarks and Gale and Greenhaven Press are registered trademarks used herein under license.

For more information, contact:
Greenhaven Press
27500 Drake Rd.
Farmington Hills, MI 48331-3535
Or you can visit our Internet site at http://www.gale.com

LIBRARY OF CONGRESS CATALOGING-IN-PUBLICATION DATA

America's global influence / David M. Haugen and Susan Musser, book editors.
  p. cm. -- (Opposing viewpoints)
  Includes bibliographical references and index.
  ISBN-13: 978-0-7377-3423-2 (hardcover)
  ISBN-10: 0-7377-3423-X (hardcover)
  ISBN-13: 978-0-7377-3424-9 (paperback)
  ISBN-10: 0-7377-3424-8 (paperback)
  1. United States--Foreign relations--2001---Juvenile literature. 2. Culture and globalization--United States--Juvenile literature. 3. Popular culture--United States--Foreign public opinion--Juvenile literature. 4. Civilization--American influences--Juvenile literature. 5. World politics--1989---Juvenile literature. I. Haugen, David M., 1969– II. Musser, Susan.
  JZ1480.A98 2007
  303.48'273--dc22
                                                                2006038045

Printed in the United States of America
10 9 8 7 6 5 4 3 2 1

Contents

Chapter 3: How Are American Economic Policies Affecting Trade and Foreign Aid?

Chapter 4: What Is the Global Impact of American Culture?

Why Consider Opposing Viewpoints?

> "The only way in which a human being can make some approach to knowing the whole of a subject is by hearing what can be said about it by persons of every variety of opinion and studying all modes in which it can be looked at by every character of mind. No wise man ever acquired his wisdom in any mode but this."
>
> John Stuart Mill

In our media-intensive culture it is not difficult to find differing opinions. Thousands of newspapers and magazines and dozens of radio and television talk shows resound with differing points of view. The difficulty lies in deciding which opinion to agree with and which "experts" seem the most credible. The more inundated we become with differing opinions and claims, the more essential it is to hone critical reading and thinking skills to evaluate these ideas. Opposing Viewpoints books address this problem directly by presenting stimulating debates that can be used to enhance and teach these skills. The varied opinions contained in each book examine many different aspects of a single issue. While examining these conveniently edited opposing views, readers can develop critical thinking skills such as the ability to compare and contrast authors' credibility, facts, argumentation styles, use of persuasive techniques, and other stylistic tools. In short, the Opposing Viewpoints series is an ideal way to attain the higher-level thinking and reading skills so essential in a culture of diverse and contradictory opinions.

In addition to providing a tool for critical thinking, Opposing Viewpoints books challenge readers to question their own strongly held opinions and assumptions. Most people form their opinions on the basis of upbringing, peer pressure, and personal, cultural, or professional bias. By reading carefully balanced opposing views, readers must directly confront new ideas as well as the opinions of those with whom they disagree. This is not to simplistically argue that everyone who reads opposing views will—or should—change his or her opinion. Instead, the series enhances readers' understanding of their own views by encouraging confrontation with opposing ideas. Careful examination of others' views can lead to the readers' understanding of the logical inconsistencies in their own opinions, perspective on why they hold an opinion, and the consideration of the possibility that their opinion requires further evaluation.

Evaluating Other Opinions

To ensure that this type of examination occurs, Opposing Viewpoints books present all types of opinions. Prominent spokespeople on different sides of each issue as well as well-known professionals from many disciplines challenge the reader. An additional goal of the series is to provide a forum for other, less known, or even unpopular viewpoints. The opinion of an ordinary person who has had to make the decision to cut off life support from a terminally ill relative, for example, may be just as valuable and provide just as much insight as a medical ethicist's professional opinion. The editors have two additional purposes in including these less known views. One, the editors encourage readers to respect others' opinions—even when not enhanced by professional credibility. It is only by reading or listening to and objectively evaluating others' ideas that one can determine whether they are worthy of consideration. Two, the inclusion of such viewpoints encourages the important critical thinking skill of objectively evaluating an author's credentials and bias. This evaluation will illuminate an author's reasons for taking a particular stance on an issue and will aid in readers' evaluation of the author's ideas.

It is our hope that these books will give readers a deeper understanding of the issues debated and an appreciation of the complexity of even seemingly simple issues when good and honest people disagree. This awareness is particularly important in a democratic society such as ours in which people enter into public debate to determine the common good. Those with whom one disagrees should not be regarded as enemies but rather as people whose views deserve careful examination and may shed light on one's own.

Thomas Jefferson once said that "difference of opinion leads to inquiry, and inquiry to truth." Jefferson, a broadly educated man, argued that "if a nation expects to be ignorant and free . . . it expects what never was and never will be." As individuals and as a nation, it is imperative that we consider the opinions of others and examine them with skill and discernment. The Opposing Viewpoints series is intended to help readers achieve this goal.

David L. Bender and Bruno Leone,
Founders

Introduction

> *"In the end, American exceptionalism, all that it is and all that it isn't, is what shapes attitudes toward the United States around the world."*
>
> —*Andrew Kohut and Bruce Stokes,*
> America Against the World

Since the collapse of the Soviet Union in 1991, the United States has emerged as the sole global superpower. Whereas once America could claim that it involved itself in foreign wars, enacted stringent diplomatic and trade policies, and spread capitalist culture to counter the threat of Communist expansion, the post–Cold War America had no ideological rivalry to easily justify furthering its interests around the world. The United States eventually gained a new opponent in 2001, after Middle Eastern terrorists attacked it on American soil by flying jet airliners into New York's World Trade Center and the Pentagon in Washington, D.C. President George W. Bush asserted that the country's new mission was to defeat terrorism and bring democracy to those parts of the world where oppressive governments sheltered the type of anti-American elements that were responsible for the 2001 tragedies. The administration's successive wars in Afghanistan and Iraq, however, seem to be making little headway against the shadowy terrorist organizations, and critics accuse the president of having ulterior motives—such as the securing of Iraqi oil fields—for pursuing war in the Middle East. These critics—from both America and abroad—argue that the United States is acting imperialistically, fearing no challenge to its right to direct world events to suit its own desires.

In addition to stating that American military ventures are examples of U.S. hard-power imperialism, critics of America's power also point to the export of trade and culture as evidence of empire building. They contend that pushing American goods, pop music, films, and television on the rest of the world is a form of soft-power warfare, or cultural imperialism. The purpose of this soft power is to persuade foreign countries to want what America has to offer—from the latest trends in clothing styles to venerated cultural values such as democracy and freedom. Some critics are already convinced that America culturally dominates the rest of the world and can dictate what it pleases. Francesco Sisci, for example, wrote in a 2002 article for the *Asia Times*,

> The US has won it all, so much so that there is not even any real resistance against soft war, despite some botched attempts to create competing cultural industries. Hollywood and its US clones dominate the cultural industry. . . . The whole information industry is dominated by Anglo-American news. No TV network or newswire is as comprehensive and persuasive as the Anglo-American ones. . . . America is so successful that everybody would like to become American.

Sisci, however, goes on to say that cultural imperialism creates its own perils. He warns, "It is impossible for America to grant the American dream to all people who dream it, either in the US or abroad. The danger of creating a desire that cannot be satisfied—whether desire for a certain product or a certain civilization—is the backlash that will follow." In Sisci's view, the backlash has manifested in increased dislike of U.S. imperialism and growing support for anti-American terrorism.

Proponents of America's hard-power and soft-power wars, on the other hand, believe that America is right to exert its influence in foreign lands. As David Rothkop argues in a well-known 1997 *Foreign Policy* article praising American cultural imperialism, "The United States should not hesitate to promote its values. In an effort to be polite or politic, Americans should not deny the fact that of all the nations in the history of the world, theirs is the most just, the most tolerant, the most willing to constantly reassess and improve itself, and the best model for the future." Such arguments rely on a belief that American virtues such as liberty, democracy, and freedom of choice are what all people yearn to acquire and that to thwart the spread of these ideas—whether through foreign policy or cultural imperialism—would be tantamount to denying oppressed people the hope that they can achieve a better life. Also implicit in these arguments for American leadership in the new world order is a faith that the United States is a benevolent empire. As Michael Mandelbaum writes in a 2006 issue of *Foreign Policy*, "In contrast with empires of the past . . . , the United States does not control, or aspire to control, directly or indirectly, the politics and economics of other societies." Viewed under this perspective, the wars in Iraq and Afghanistan are conducted with the intent of stopping dictatorial regimes that aid terrorists and threaten not only U.S. interests but the interests of all people in the free world. America therefore must always stand up to global bullies or lose its rightful place as the defender of democracy and free markets.

While critics may debate the pros and cons of America's influence on the global stage, there are some forecasters who claim that U.S. dominance is far from assured. The National Intelligence Council published a report in 2005 that predicts America "will see its relative power erode" in the coming decades. The report argues that "rising Asia will continue to reshape globalisation, giving it less of a 'Made in the USA' character and more of an Asian look and feel." This prediction rests greatly on China's booming economy, which is earning six dollars in exports to America for every one dollar China spends on U.S. imports. Other commentators suggest that globalization—especially cultural globalization—has never been very one-sided in the first place. In an issue of the *International Economy*, Philippe Legrain claims "it is a myth that globalization involves the imposition of Americanized uniformity, rather than an explosion of cultural exchange." To Legrain, globalized culture borrows what is universally appealing from a wide variety of regional sources. He also asserts that "globalization is not a one-way street. . . . Foreigners are changing America even as they adopt its ways." As observers note, this cross-fertilization has been aided by the Internet and other telecommunications media, which have liberated people worldwide from the confines of geography. With these technologies in place, it becomes easier for individuals to sample from a variety of cultures so that all people—including Americans—become more broadly globalized instead of simply Americanized.

The authors in *Opposing Viewpoints: America's Global Influence* address both the nation's hard-power and soft-power strategies in chapters titled: What Are the Aims and Impact of America's Foreign Policy Agenda? How Are U.S. Military Policies Affecting America's Global Influence? How Are American Economic Policies Affecting Trade and Foreign Aid? What Is the Global Impact of American Culture? Some of these authors view America's power as waxing, while others contend that it is waning, but all acknowledge that the nation has been exceptional in shaping world events, orchestrating global economies, and selling its image—and perhaps its values—to a mostly receptive world audience.

CHAPTER 1

What Are the Aims and Impact of America's Foreign Policy Agenda?

Chapter Preface

In a commencement speech given June 1, 2002, before the graduates of the U.S. Military Academy at West Point, President George W. Bush put forth a new agenda for U.S. foreign policy that has come to be known as the Bush Doctrine. According to the Bush Doctrine, America and its allies are facing a new global threat in the forms of terrorism and rogue nations bent on obtaining weapons of mass destruction. The president declared that the United States would meet these threats with the force of America's overwhelming military superiority. He made it clear that the nation would not wait to be a victim of terrorist acts or attacks by weapons of mass destruction; instead, America would exercise preemptive military engagement to defuse such threats before they could be carried out.

In addition to countering terrorism through armed force, the Bush Doctrine gave the nation a mission "to promote moderation and tolerance and human rights." America would carry out this mission by supporting those around the world who are seeking to establish democratic reform in the midst of oppressive tyrannies. While a noble cause in its own right, the effort to promote freedom and democracy in other lands is also a component of the strategy to thwart global terrorism; that is, in theory, the motivations for terrorism will not survive in countries opened up to democratic institutions and the rule of law.

The Bush Doctrine has had many proponents and detractors. Chief among the concerns has been the willingness of the administration to act unilaterally to promote the doctrine's dual aims. Although the president reaffirmed America's commitment to seek multilateral counsel before exercising U.S. military might, the war in Iraq has shown that the United States is willing to proceed with only limited international support. Some members of the administration, including the vice president and the secretary of defense, however, contend that America has a duty to act unilaterally if the threat is great enough and multinational efforts are ineffective. The authors in the following chapter debate the charges of American unilateralism as well as other aspects of the nation's new foreign policy agenda.

| *"The world's problems will not be re-
solved by the unilateral use of force."*

America's Unilateralism Aggravates Global Problems

Robert F. Drinan

Jesuit Father Robert F. Drinan is a professor at Georgetown University Law Center. In the following viewpoint Drinan argues that the administration of George W. Bush is exacerbating global tensions by behaving like a rogue superpower. Instead of seeking international cooperation in global matters, Drinan says, the Bush administration is defying international law and making enemies as it pursues an imperialist agenda based on its military superiority.

As you read, consider the following questions:

1. According to Drinan, what three weapons conventions has the Bush administration withdrawn from or refused to take part in?

2. What aspects of the Bush doctrine does Drinan mention in his condemnation of the administration's defense policy?

Robert F. Drinan, "Bush's Unilateralism Aggravates World's Problems," *National Catholic Reporter*, vol. 31, January 10, 2003, p. 16. Copyright © 2003 The National Catholic Reporter Publishing Company, 115 E. Armour Blvd., Kansas City, MO 64111. All rights reserved. Reproduced by permission of *National Catholic Reporter*, www.natcath.org.

3. According to Jimmy Carter, as cited by Drinan, what is the most serious and universal global problem?

In the [first] 24 months of the [George W.] Bush administration, America's foreign policy has become confused and incoherent because of a new and indefensible unilateralism. The United States has more and more isolated itself from international law and from the accumulated wisdom of the arms control community.

The most recent example of the "Lone Ranger" mentality is the announcement by the White House that it will return to the idea of creating a shield in the sky against incoming missiles. This concept, created by President [Ronald] Reagan as "Star Wars," has never worked and is not needed since the demise of the "Evil Empire" [as Reagan called the Soviet Union] in 1990.

But this missile defense scheme is just the most recent instance of the United States rejecting world opinion. In 2001 President Bush announced that the United States would withdraw from the 1972 Anti–Ballistic Missile (ABM) Treaty and that the United States would once again resume nuclear explosions. In doing so the United States took a step opposed by Russia, China and most U.S. allies.

The Bush administration has also walked out of the biological weapons convention agreed to by 143 nations. Similarly, the United States refused to sign the treaty barring antipersonnel land mines even though every country in the western hemisphere except Cuba signed it along with every NATO [North Atlantic Treaty Organization] country except Turkey.

The United States has also defied the concerns of the world on limiting the transfer of small weapons. The United States continues to be the number one manufacturer of weapons of war, including the sale of small weapons.

An Imperialist Nation Disregarding International Law

The unilateralism of the United States was visible once again when President Bush shocked the rest of the world by withdrawing from the Kyoto Global Warming Treaty agreed to by 178 other countries. The United States also followed its self-proclaimed unilateralism when it refused to ratify the International Criminal Court.

The defiance of international law is also present in the new Bush doctrine of preemptive military action. The White House relies on the attacks of Sept. 11 as justification of a preemptive strike in the absence of any evidence of an imminent attack. The Bush doctrine seems to support a position that America's unique military preeminence excuses it from obeying the rules of international law. The administration is calling for an American imperialism that must be carried out with little regard for the United Nations or the long-standing doctrines of international law.

The Bush doctrine wrongly assumes that massive military power can keep the United States safe. In the first two years of the Bush administration the military budget has been increased by some 30 percent. The defense budget has $385 billion dollars to spend—a sum larger than all of the other nations of the world put together. The United States now spends over $1 billion a day on the military!

I have followed arms control since the 1960s. I wrote a book on this subject and taught courses on it at Georgetown University for many years. Never before has an administration defied the accumulated wisdom of arms controllers and rejected the treaties agreed upon by all of the major nations.

Using Reckless Force in the Name of World Peace

Representatives of the president and the Pentagon have, in the name of fighting terrorism, revived some of the worst ideas

U.S. Arrogance Exceeds Self-Interest

In advance of launching the war in Iraq, America's explicit message to other governments on the UN Security Council was that the position they adopted would not determine whether there would be a war. That had already been decided. The only consequences of their vote would be in showing whether they were on the side of the United States and whether the United Nations would back a war that would take place because the United States had decided it would take place. The debate would show, as President [George W.] Bush declared in the immediate aftermath of September 11, [2001,] whether others were with the United States or with the terrorists. It was not the approach that was best calculated to obtain a Security Council resolution endorsing the war. Yet manifesting nationalist disdain for multilateralism seemed to take precedence over the Bush administration's interest in obtaining Security Council sanction for the war.

Since September 11, the Bush Administration has seemed to relish its opportunities to demonstrate that international agreements, whether it is [the] Kyoto [environmental protocol] or the treaty establishing the International Criminal Court, or a host of others, cannot bind it. It has shown contempt for international public opinion. . . . It has exceeded what would be required if it were merely acting in self-interest.

Aryeh Neier, "America's New Nationalism
(Part IV: What We Gain, What We Lose: The Effects of Fear),"
Social Research, vol. 71, no. 4, Winter 2004.

engendered by the Cold War. They have intimidated the people from speaking out. The . . . war in Iraq will in all probability further silence even those who know that the new military posture is not grounded in reality, but in a war-mongering crusade based on the illusion that military might can subdue the terrorists and bring peace to the world.

One can only wonder what the 1.2 billion people in 48 Islamic nations think as the United States invades Afghanistan and now Iraq. Ten or 20 years from now what will the Islamic world think of a United States that uses weapons of mass destruction to achieve supremacy?

The Bush White House has clearly misjudged the problems of the world. It has assumed that the unilateral threat and use of barbarous weapons will guarantee American supremacy and thus world peace.

The world's problems will not be resolved by the unilateral use of force. President [Jimmy] Carter put it well. In his speech accepting the Nobel Peace Prize he wisely saw that "the most serious and universal problem is the growing chasm between the richest and the poorest people on earth." President Carter continued: "The results of this disparity are root causes of most of the world's unresolved problems, including starvation, illiteracy, environmental degradation, violent conflict and unnecessary illnesses that range from Guinea worm to HIV/ AIDS."

It is painful to have to note that the Bush administration and the Pentagon have not recognized these truths and as a result are aggravating these problems by threatening violence and war. There is no solution to this problem except a moral revolution by millions of people who are ashamed and angry at the policies their nation has advocated.

> *"What the United States brings to the world stage can hardly be cast as unilateralism. Rather, we bring leadership."*

America Does Not Act Unilaterally

Paula J. Dobriansky

Paula J. Dobriansky is the undersecretary of state for global affairs. In the following viewpoint she counters accusations that America's foreign policy is unilateral—that is, that the United States favors acting on its own to further its own interests rather than submitting to multinational efforts to address global problems. Dobriansky argues that the U.S government has always favored multilateral alliances to respond to military threats, economic disparity, and health crises. She acknowledges, however, that because America is the driving force of global democracy, much of the nation's leadership in foreign relations has been misconstrued as unilateralism.

As you read, consider the following questions:

1. What does Dobriansky mean when she says about the war on terror, "While multilateralism is our first resort, it cannot and will not be our last resort"?

Paula J. Dobriansky, "Unilateralism and U.S. Foreign Policy," remarks to Woodrow Wilson School of International and Public Affairs, Princeton University, Princeton, New Jersey, December 5, 2003. www.state.gov.

2. In the author's view, how does U.S. economic policy refute accusations of unilateralism?

3. According to Dobriansky, in what way does the U.S. government consider the Kyoto Protocol flawed?

Unilateralism, in the pejorative sense . . . , is something quite distinct from U.S. power as it is exercised today. Unilateralism, properly construed, connotes reckless indifference to, if not contempt for, the needs and concerns of others. This applies to an Iraq under Saddam Hussein, who coveted the wealth of his neighbors at terrible cost. This describes a North Korea under Kim Jong Il, who has brandished nuclear arms to extort aid from the world community. More broadly, it characterizes the despots who have referred to nothing but their own appetites and the limits of their armies as a guide to their conduct in world affairs.

American conduct is entirely different. Yes, the United States is a great nation, wielding enormous power. But we owe our greatness not to the force of arms, but to the force of ideas: our rule of law, our freedom of commerce, and most of all, our freedom to unleash the creative abilities and talents that have flourished for so long within our democratic system. Ideas are the source of America's health, wealth, and power.

Leadership, Not Unilateralism

America's tremendous respect for the dignity and rights of the individual brings with it a recognition of the rights of all humanity, not only within our borders, but beyond. As President [George W.] Bush said in his speech at Whitehall Palace in London on November 19th [2003], our deepest beliefs "set the direction of our foreign policy. We value our own civil rights, so we stand for the human rights of others. We affirm the God-given dignity of every person, so we are moved to action by poverty and oppression and famine and disease."

What the United States brings to the world stage can hardly be cast as unilateralism. Rather, we bring leadership.

We lead in some matters by example; in others, by deliberate policy. And in the most vital issue of our time—the defense and progress of the free world—we lead because we must. It is derived from our character as a free people. We did not set out to become a superpower. We set out to be a nation of liberty and justice for all, and in so doing, we found ourselves manning the front lines of the democratic world.

That has had its tough moments. It is now 60 years since [former British prime minister] Winston Churchill, speaking in time of war at Harvard University, reminded Americans that "The price of greatness is responsibility." He noted that "one cannot rise to be in so many ways the leading community in the civilized world without being involved in its problems, without being convulsed by its agonies and inspired by its causes." . . .

The United States Has Not Acted Alone

Now, in one of the principal challenges of our time, the War on Terror, we have again taken up our responsibilities, and while multilateralism is our first resort, it cannot and will not be our last resort. Our deepest responsibility is not to the shifting currents of world opinion, swayed in some cases by dictators who would bully or bribe their way to influence. Nor are we bound in every instance to assemblies that include the voices of tyrants along with those of free men and women. Our truest obligation is to the defense of America and Americans against a foe that threatens civilization and the basic values that animate the free world.

Despite being accused of unilateralism, the United States has not acted alone. Invariably, we have sought to engage and cooperate with nations whose governments share our values. The United States has scores of partners across the globe in the war on terrorism. For example, 167 countries have issued orders freezing terrorist assets in their jurisdictions. Ninety countries have expressed support for the global war on terrorism. And America is working with many partners to rebuild Afghanistan after two decades of war and deprivation.

Next, there is the matter of Iraq. Not only did the U.S. vigorously seek the backing of the world community; we had it—in the form of 17 United Nations resolutions, including Resolution 1441, which was adopted unanimously by the Security Council in November 2002. This resolution reaffirmed that Saddam Hussein was in violation of all of the previous Security Council resolutions and called for appropriate consequences. If anything, we took those multilateral resolutions more seriously than did some other members of the U.N. Forty-eight countries joined the United States in supporting Operation Iraqi Freedom.

We sought wide counsel, we listened well, and when we finally took action to remove a dangerous dictator, we assembled a coalition of the willing. We did, in the course of that, perform an act of leadership. We acted in accord with American principles, embodied in the Universal Declaration of Human Rights, that through many decades, despite the regular bouts of doubt and debate, have wrought so much good in this world.

The United States has also cooperated with many others to consolidate and expand the territory in which the tenets of the Universal Declaration have real meaning. To this end, for example, we have worked hard with the Community of Democracies, a movement of democratic nations from around the globe—which first met [in 2000] in Warsaw, and again [in 2002] when representatives of 130 countries gathered in Seoul [Korea]. Out of these meetings have come commitments from many nations to strengthen good governance and support each other's progress by way of regional cooperation. Our role has included support for such projects as the Dialogue on Democracy, a roundtable that recently brought together govern

America Should Lead Global Alliances

At this time of such a preponderance of American power in the international system, the United States can and should build alliances and international regimes that address its central security concerns and commit to common action with those states that share its interests and willingness to address problems. The time has come to pivot the international system from one that served the interests of the United States and the vast majority of other states well in the post–World War II environment to one that will perpetuate and advance American interests into the next American-led century. It is manifestly in the U.S. interest to attract and bind other states into voluntarily supporting this international agenda. Americans may not like all those other states wringing their hands with concern about America's behavior in the world and complaining that they are essentially supporting the U.S. agenda. Imagine how much less attractive an international order would be in which the U.S. had to force the other states into going along with U.S. choices. Far better that participating states benefit from a system of accepted leadership and see that they can best advance their interests by working with a United States advancing its own.

Kori Schake and Klaus Becher, "How America Should Lead,"
Policy Review, August/September 2002.

ment and non-governmental representatives of 14 democratic nations in Latin America and Africa to share their experiences and learn from each other.

Sharing Economic Prosperity

In the matter of global prosperity, America has also labored long and hard to share wealth and alleviate poverty—not only by being the world's most generous donor to distressed nations, but also in disseminating the free-market ideas and policies that best equip people, anywhere, to help themselves and realize their full potential. At the World Trade Organization, America has long been the major, driving force for opening the world's markets, leading by example and pressing most recently a series of proposals for promoting trade in agriculture and services. The United States has also opened its own markets to poor countries through programs such as the Generalized System of Preferences, which grants duty-free treatment to over 4,000 products from more than 140 countries, and regional initiatives like the African Growth and Opportunity Act, the Andean Trade Promotion and Drug Eradication Act, and the Caribbean Basin Initiative, each of which was expanded in 2002. Were we unilateralists, we could simply walk away. We have not done that. We understand the stakes, and we have chosen over and over to press for policies that would help empower the world's poorest people to achieve the kind of prosperity we enjoy, and which we know from experience that free trade can deliver.

In the realm of aid, we provide the lion's share of support to multilateral institutions such as the World Bank and International Monetary Fund, not to mention their parent organization, the United Nations. As experience has led us to question how effective some of this aid has been in practice, we have adjusted our policies accordingly. During the Financing for Sustainable Development Conference at Monterrey [Mexico, in 2002], we led the way toward more effective help and relief for developing nations. President Bush introduced the Millennium Challenge Account, a 50% increase in core U.S. foreign assistance, linking aid to incentives for the kind of true reforms—in economic policy, good governance, and investments in the health, education and welfare of one's own population—that set people free to prosper.

We also recognize that some crises cannot wait upon the long-term goals of democratic good governance and open markets. America today leads the way in fighting one of the world's worst health crises—the global spread of HIV-AIDS—especially in Africa, where in some nations it has become the leading cause of death. . . . And while we have stepped to the fore in the fight to free Africa and other regions of this scourge, we welcome partners from all corners of the planet. The more multilateral, the better.

Addressing the Global Environmental Challenge

There are, of course, criticisms that America has been unilateral in such important matters as the environment—notably our rejection of the Kyoto Protocol on climate change. Here, again, the issue was not one of dismissing our responsibilities to the world community, but of living up to them. We see the Kyoto Protocol as flawed. It is a formula for imposing immense costs—up to $400 billion and 4.9 million jobs lost in the United States alone. Taking into account that U.S. output makes up approximately one-quarter of the global economy, and that U.S. economic vitality has a powerful impact on other economies worldwide, American implementation of Kyoto would penalize us all, with no clear gain.

At the same time, we remain an active participant in the U.N. Framework Convention on Climate Change, working with other countries to stabilize greenhouse gas concentrations at a level that will prevent dangerous human interference with the climate. We have also put forward a number of practical initiatives, engaging the global community to protect the environment. In fact, the United States has bilateral agreements addressing climate change with eleven countries and two regional organizations, including the European Union. Our concern has been that any sweeping moves be based on good science and a reasonable understanding of how the costs and benefits might balance out. Beyond that, America's position is to defend and promote the kind of democratic, free-market systems in which citizens not only desire a cleaner, greener, better environment, but actually enjoy the political power and economic resources to achieve those goals. . . .

America Shoulders the Burden of Leadership

On all these fronts, America can be charged with defending first and foremost our own interests. To that, we can with honor plead guilty. It is precisely our own freedoms that have handed us the might and wealth to stand as the world's superpower—but endowed us also with the compassion, generosity and wisdom to see that these blessings are best preserved among our own citizens if they are enjoyed by others as well. With every move, we seek ways to expand their reach and to forge a world community of free nations, in which all honest partners are deeply welcome. . . .

We also recognize that America cannot be a global leader unless others are willingly led. The National Security Strategy released in September 2002 clearly states that "no nation can build a safer, better world alone. Alliances and multilateral institutions can multiply the strength of freedom-loving nations."

Of course, building and leading alliances is not simple. And the making of free nations takes great will and much work. But the direction has been clear. So has the desire of America, its government and its people, to stand by the beliefs that have made this country great, a leader among nations. Time and again, we have shouldered the responsibilities this brings. In years ahead, it is not a path of unilateralism that history will record. The time will come when scholars at this fine school [Princeton] will look back on these days as an era in which, at crucial moments, the U.S. took necessary steps toward a world in which all nations might share in the responsibilities, and the greatness, of free peoples.

> *"The best hope for peace in our world is the expansion of freedom in all the world."*

America Is Committed to Promoting Democracy Throughout the World

George W. Bush

George W. Bush is the forty-third president of the United States. In the following viewpoint, taken from his second inaugural address in 2005, Bush states that America must work to spread liberty and democracy throughout the world. The United States has always been a beacon for oppressed people around the globe, Bush says, and the nation must seek to end tyranny wherever it remains. This mission, Bush argues, is as important for America's own security as it is for bringing peace to the rest of the world.

As you read, consider the following questions:

1. Why does Bush contend that spreading democracy is not "primarily the task of arms"?
2. What choice does the president say that America will give to "every ruler and every nation"?
3. According to Bush, how will America "encourage" reform in foreign governments?

George W. Bush, second inaugural address, January 20, 2005. www.whitehouse.gov.

There is only one force of history that can break the reign of hatred and resentment [in the world], and expose the pretensions of tyrants, and reward the hopes of the decent and tolerant, and that is the force of human freedom.

We are led, by events and common sense, to one conclusion: The survival of liberty in our land increasingly depends on the success of liberty in other lands. The best hope for peace in our world is the expansion of freedom in all the world.

America's vital interests and our deepest beliefs are now one. From the day of our Founding, we have proclaimed that every man and woman on this earth has rights, and dignity, and matchless value, because they bear the image of the Maker of Heaven and earth. Across the generations we have proclaimed the imperative of self-government, because no one is fit to be a master, and no one deserves to be a slave. Advancing these ideals is the mission that created our Nation. It is the honorable achievement of our fathers. Now it is the urgent requirement of our nation's security, and the calling of our time.

So it is the policy of the United States to seek and support the growth of democratic movements and institutions in every nation and culture, with the ultimate goal of ending tyranny in our world. This is not primarily the task of arms, though we will defend ourselves and our friends by force of arms when necessary. Freedom, by its nature, must be chosen, and defended by citizens, and sustained by the rule of law and the protection of minorities. And when the soul of a nation finally speaks, the institutions that arise may reflect customs and traditions very different from our own. America will not impose our own style of government on the unwilling. Our goal instead is to help others find their own voice, attain their own freedom, and make their own way.

The U.S. Objectives for Spreading Democracy

The great objective of ending tyranny is the concentrated work of generations. The difficulty of the task is no excuse for avoiding it. America's influence is not unlimited, but fortunately for the oppressed, America's influence is considerable, and we will use it confidently in freedom's cause. . . .

We will persistently clarify the choice before every ruler and every nation: The moral choice between oppression, which is always wrong, and freedom, which is eternally right. America will not pretend that jailed dissidents prefer their chains, or that women welcome humiliation and servitude, or that any human being aspires to live at the mercy of bullies.

We will encourage reform in other governments by making clear that success in our relations will require the decent treatment of their own people. America's belief in human dignity will guide our policies, yet rights must be more than the grudging concessions of dictators; they are secured by free dissent and the participation of the governed. In the long run, there is no justice without freedom, and there can be no human rights without human liberty.

Some, I know, have questioned the global appeal of liberty—though this time in history, four decades defined by the swiftest advance of freedom ever seen, is an odd time for doubt. Americans, of all people, should never be surprised by the power of our ideals. Eventually, the call of freedom comes to every mind and every soul. We do not accept the existence of permanent tyranny because we do not accept the possibility of permanent slavery. Liberty will come to those who love it.

America's Pledge

Today, America speaks anew to the peoples of the world:

All who live in tyranny and hopelessness can know: the United States will not ignore your oppression, or excuse your oppressors. When you stand for your liberty, we will stand with you.

The More Democracies, the Better

Overall, the expansion of democracy over the past three decades has been a net gain not only for the United States but also for the world as a whole.

The near absence of wars among mature liberal democracies—perhaps the most robust finding in international relations research today—means that democratic states need not prepare for war against one another. This allows them to invest resources elsewhere that might have been used on such preparations.

Democracies reap other efficiency gains as well. They are evidently more likely to trade with and invest in one another, which tends to raise their rates of productivity growth. More generally, their institutions make them relatively transparent and constrained, Which in turn allows them to reach more efficient bargains with one another, with less hedging than afflicts relations among non-democracies. Thus they are more likely voluntarily to join and abide by international agreements than other types of states, and to form and maintain effective regional organizations that pool power. . . .

Taken together, these advantages mean that, broadly speaking, the more democracies there are in the world, the better off is each democracy.

John M. Owen IV, "Democracy, Realistically,"
National Interest, *Spring 2006.*

Democratic reformers facing repression, prison, or exile can know: America sees you for who you are: the future leaders of your free country.

The rulers of outlaw regimes can know that we still believe as Abraham Lincoln did: "Those who deny freedom to others deserve it not for themselves; and, under the rule of a just God, cannot long retain it."

The leaders of governments with long habits of control need to know: To serve your people you must learn to trust them. Start on this journey of progress and justice, and America will walk at your side.

And all the allies of the United States can know: we honor your friendship, we rely on your counsel, and we depend on your help. Division among free nations is a primary goal of freedom's enemies. The concerted effort of free nations to promote democracy is a prelude to our enemies' defeat.

Today, I also speak anew to my fellow citizens:

From all of you, I have asked patience in the hard task of securing America, which you have granted in good measure. Our country has accepted obligations that are difficult to fulfill, and would be dishonorable to abandon. Yet because we have acted in the great liberating tradition of this nation, tens of millions have achieved their freedom. And as hope kindles hope, millions more will find it. . . .

From the perspective of a single day, including this day of dedication, the issues and questions before our country are many. From the viewpoint of centuries, the questions that come to us are narrowed and few. Did our generation advance the cause of freedom? And did our character bring credit to that cause?

Confidence in the Triumph of Freedom

These questions that judge us also unite us, because Americans of every party and background, Americans by choice and by birth, are bound to one another in the cause of freedom. We have known divisions, which must be healed to move forward in great purposes—and I will strive in good faith to heal them. Yet those divisions do not define America. We felt the unity and fellowship of our nation when freedom came under attack, and our response came like a single hand over a single heart. And we can feel that same unity and pride whenever America acts for good, and the victims of disaster are given hope, and the unjust encounter justice, and the captives are set free.

We go forward with complete confidence in the eventual triumph of freedom. Not because history runs on the wheels of inevitability; it is human choices that move events. Not because we consider ourselves a chosen nation; God moves and chooses as He wills. We have confidence because freedom is the permanent hope of mankind, the hunger in dark places, the longing of the soul. When our Founders declared a new order of the ages; when soldiers died in wave upon wave for a union based on liberty; when citizens marched in peaceful outrage under the banner "Freedom Now"—they were acting on an ancient hope that is meant to be fulfilled. History has an ebb and flow of justice, but history also has a visible direction, set by liberty and the Author of Liberty.

When the Declaration of Independence was first read in public and the Liberty Bell was sounded in celebration, a witness said, "It rang as if it meant something." In our time it means something still. America, in this young century, proclaims liberty throughout all the world, and to all the inhabitants thereof. Renewed in our strength—tested, but not weary—we are ready for the greatest achievements in the history of freedom.

"Promoting democracy means more than basking in the glow of American idealism."

America Is Not Committed to Promoting Democracy Throughout the World

Joseph T. Siegle and Morton H. Halperin

In the following viewpoint Joseph T. Siegle and Morton H. Halperin argue that the George W. Bush administration has professed to support global democracy but has failed to live up to its word. According to the authors, the administration has backed dictators, defied independence movements, and pursued its war on terror at the expense of building democracy. Siegle and Halperin claim that the false rhetoric is damaging U.S. credibility, especially in the Arab world where reformers have seen that the democratization of Iraq and Afghanistan has meant U.S. invasion and years of occupation. Siegle researches global trends in democracy at the University of Maryland. Halperin is the U.S. advocacy director for the Open Society Institute.

Joseph T. Siegle and Morton H. Halperin, "Bush's Rhetoric Battles with His Policies; Promoting Democracy," *International Herald Tribune*, February 8, 2005, p. 8. Copyright © 2005 *International Herald Tribune*. Reprinted with permission of the authors.

As you read, consider the following questions:

1. According to Siegle and Halperin, the Bush administration was the only government in the Western Hemisphere to recognize an ill-fated coup attempt in what country?

2. As the authors state, what priorities superseded effective democracy building in Afghanistan?

3. In what way has "American democracy promotion . . . come to be defined as the invasion of Iraq," in the words of Siegle and Halperin?

As at his inaugural, the theme of freedom again figured prominently in George W. Bush's [2005] State of the Union address. This would seem to confirm the seismic transformation of an administration that arrived in Washington four years ago [in 2001] mocking the very notion of democracy promotion. Neoconservatives are delighted, while traditional security conservatives scoff at the idea of democracy as a centerpiece of U.S. foreign policy.

The reactions of both camps are misplaced, however. For despite his stirring rhetoric, the reality is that Bush simply doesn't have a very strong record of promoting democracy abroad. During his first term, Bush praised the democratic visions of Vladimir Putin and Pervez Musharraf as they systematically smothered the embers of freedom in Russia and Pakistan [respectively]. This is the president that stood shoulder to shoulder with the Chinese prime minister, Wen Jiabao, while publicly condemning a proposed referendum on independence in democratic Taiwan.

This is the same administration that was the only government in the Western Hemisphere to recognize the ill-fated coup attempt against the democratically elected leader in Venezuela. Despite its democratic pronouncements, this administration remains a steadfast supporter of entrenched autocrats in Egypt, Saudi Arabia and Central Asia.

Even in Iraq and Afghanistan, places that Bush's supporters point to as examples of his commitment to advancing freedom, the evidence is dubious.

The Problems in Iraq and Afghanistan

Leaving aside the irony of invading a country to "bring it democracy," Bush nodded to the Department of Defense to take the lead in the democracy-building effort in Iraq. Their plan: Install Ahmed Chalabi as the new Iraqi leader. The U.S. has been scrambling in Iraq ever since.

Coming nearly two years after the invasion, the recent elections are an important step toward creating a degree of legitimacy within Iraq's political leadership. This accomplishment, however, has come at considerable cost in lives lost, stability and American prestige—costs that could have been mitigated if a commitment to prepare for a democratic transition had been made a priority.

In Afghanistan, the Bush administration sided with the country's powerful warlords at the expense of the new central government—a choice deemed necessary to track down the Taliban [reactionary religious government of Afghanistan] and al Qaeda [terrorists behind the September 11, 2001, attacks on America] leadership. Similarly, the administration's commitment to democracy didn't extend to supporting an expansion of the international security force beyond Kabul. And despite the elections there, insecurity remains the predominate theme in the country.

The Democracy Smokescreen

The essential point is that establishing democracy was not the rationale for these military interventions. It has always been an after-the-fact justification for other priorities—capturing [al Qaeda's leader] Osama bin Laden, destroying al Qaeda and the Taliban, and eliminating [Iraqi dictator] Saddam Hussein's control of weapons of mass destruction.

Democracy Will Not Come Easy to the Middle East

President [George W.] Bush's notions that democratizing Iraq will have a ripple effect on the rest of the Arab world—bringing prosperity and peace to the region—and that democracy is the panacea for Islamic terrorism are unsubstantiated and misleading. Even a cursory review of the Arab political landscape indicates that the rise of democracy in the Arab states will not translate automatically into the establishment of liberal democracies. In fact, given the opportunity to compete freely and fairly in an election, Islamists will most likely emerge as the winners. And if current sentiments in the Arab states offer a guide, any government formed by elected Islamist political parties will be more antagonistic to the United States than are current authoritarian regimes. In addition, there are no indications that democracy is a prerequisite to defeating terrorism or any empirical data to support the claim of links existing between authoritarian regimes and terrorism.

Alon Ben-Meir, "Democracy of Convenience?"
American Chronicle, *November 7, 2005.*
www.americanchronicle.com.

Rather than a democratic idealist, Bush is better described as someone who has co-opted the language of democracy while pursuing business-as-usual policies. While politically expedient, this confounding strategy carries considerable risks.

First, it distracts Americans from addressing some of the very priorities Bush trumpeted in his speech. Peace and prosperity elsewhere in the world do contribute to U.S. security. Democratic governments do a far better job, on average, of generating improved standards of living and avoiding conflict.

Second, promulgating the rhetoric without pursuing the requisite policies sets a democracy-based foreign policy up for failure. Little is done to advance democracy around the world, while "realists," like former U.S. National Security Adviser Brent Scowcroft, can blame the shortcomings of Bush's foreign policy on the ideological weaknesses of a democracy-oriented approach. Heads, realists win; tails, democracy promoters lose.

Third, the disconnect between rhetoric and reality has stirred up deep suspicions of established means of democracy promotion. The credibility of efforts to strengthen the capacity of reformers and build real democratic institutions are undermined. Instead, American democracy promotion has come to be defined as the invasion of Iraq. And the lawlessness, the destruction, the emergence of terrorism and the foreign occupation that are associated with this package are a tough sell for democratic reformers in the Arab world or elsewhere.

Fourth, hollow oratory only corrodes perceptions of U.S. credibility in pursuit of its principles. The effect is to weaken the United States' ability to lead in its strategic aim of shaping global norms of democracy, the rule of law, tolerance, nonproliferation of illicit weaponry and the illegitimacy of terrorism.

Masking American Opportunism

Promoting democracy means more than basking in the glow of American idealism. It requires consistently backing, in word and deed, those who are fighting to see it realized. Better not to say anything than to make idealistic pronouncements that have no bearing on U.S. actions. Otherwise, democracy promotion will come to be understood as American opportunism rather than a genuine desire to see more of the world's citizens gain control over their destiny. America's credibility is a precious commodity. Americans wear it out at their own peril.

Periodical Bibliography

The following articles have been selected to supplement the diverse views presented in this chapter.

Ivo H. Daalder and James M. Lindsay	"Bush's Flawed Revolution: 'If We're an Arrogant Nation,' Said George W. Bush, 'They'll Resent Us.' He Was Right," *American Prospect*, November 2003.
Chuck Hagel	"Defining America's Role on the Global Stage," *USA Today* magazine, May 2003.
Michael A. Ledeen	"The Advance of Freedom: US Foreign Policy and Democratic Revolution," *Harvard International Review*, Spring 2005.
Clyde Prestowitz	"Losing Friends & Alienating People: U.S. Diplomats and Policy Experts of All Political Stripes Agree: Bush's Unilateralist Policies Have Been Disastrous to Our Own Interests," *Mother Jones*, May/June 2004.
Doug Saunders	"The Fourth World War: For Two Years, the U.S. Has Pursued the Culprits Behind the 9/11 Atrocities with a Vengeance That Has Shocked and Awed Ally and Enemy Alike," *Toronto Globe & Mail*, September 6, 2003.
Kori Schake and Klaus Becher	"How America Should Lead," *Policy Review*, August/September 2002.
John L. Scherer	"America on the Defensive," *USA Today* magazine, July 2005.
Sherle R. Schwenninger	"A World Neglected: The Foreign Policy Debate We Should Be Having," *Nation*, October 18, 2004.
Stephen M. Walt	"Taming American Power," *Foreign Affairs*, September/October 2005.

OPPOSING
VIEWPOINTS®
SERIES

CHAPTER 2

How Are U.S. Military Policies Affecting America's Global Influence?

Chapter Preface

In 1985, North Korea signed the Non-Proliferation Treaty (NPT), promising not to pursue any further development of nuclear technology for military and domestic use. In January 2003, North Korea, under the leadership of Kim Jong Il, withdrew from the NPT after admitting to covertly pursuing nuclear aims. The United States has no proof that North Korea possesses any nuclear weapons, but the administration of President George W. Bush maintains that North Korea's nuclear goals are a potential threat to the rest of the world. Since diplomatic relations and economic sanctions failed in the past to halt North Korea's nuclear aspirations, many analysts are debating whether the administration should employ military force to prevent Kim Jong-Il's regime from further enhancing its nuclear weapons capabilities.

Proponents of employing military force to intervene have most often advocated a limited line of attack. Ashton B. Carter and William J. Perry proposed in an article in the *Washington Post* in 2006 that if North Korea plans to test ballistic missiles capable of carrying nuclear weapons, the United States must destroy the missiles prior to testing. Carter and Perry suggested that any U.S. attack plan should target only missile development sites, and they advised that the North Koreans be forewarned of the coming attacks so the government could evacuate civilians and avoid needless casualties.

Suggestions of restricted and careful military intervention come in response to numerous critics who cite various reasons why military involvement should be avoided. Phillip Saunders, writing for the Center for Nonproliferation Studies in 2003, argued that due to the hidden nature of the North Korean nuclear facilities and their underground location, U.S. strikes against such targets had a possibility of yielding only insignificant results. Further, he warns that these attacks could incite harmful retaliation strikes against U.S. troops and allies, counteracting any gains made by a preemptive U.S. attack.

No military intervention has been employed against North Korea since the Korean War, and Bush maintains that a U.S. attack remains a last-resort option. The Bush administration and previous presidential administrations, though, have used America's military might to further U.S. interests and respond to perceived threats. The authors in the following chapter present a wide range of views concerning U.S. military intervention as a tool of foreign policy.

| "The existence of a powerful and battle-proven military makes the job of diplomats and political leaders vastly easier."

U.S. Foreign Policy Should Use Military Strength to Support Diplomacy

Frederick W. Kagan

Frederick W. Kagan asserts in the following viewpoint that diplomacy and military force are complementary tools of foreign policy. He contends that using military force to achieve a political objective can often be more effective and expedient than following unproductive diplomatic channels. Force, however, has to be used justly and wisely, Kagan argues, but it also must be employed decisively. The United States used decisive force in Iraq, for example, to thwart Saddam Hussein's expansionist plans. According to Kagan, America must continue to underpin its diplomacy with a credible military threat so that even the most obstinate foreign powers will take U.S. policy measures seriously. Kagan is a scholar in defense and security studies at the American Enterprise Institute.

Frederick W. Kagan, "Power and Persuasion," *The Wilson Quarterly*, vol. 29, no. 3, summer 2005, pp. 57-65. Copyright © 2005 Woodrow Wilson International Center for Scholars. Reproduced by permission.

As you read, consider the following questions:

1. Why does Kagan believe that spreading democracy in the Middle East is a worthwhile and achievable goal for the United States?

2. According to the author, in what way was the U.S. response to Iraqi aggression different from Britain's response to the Italian occupation of Corfu?

3. Why does Kagan believe that stirring anger and resentment in an enemy population is not a reason to reject military action against a rival nation?

"You have no idea how much it contributes to the general politeness and pleasantness of diplomacy when you have a little quiet armed force in the background," the diplomat-historian George F. Kennan declared in 1946. With his customary wit, Kennan enunciated a profound general principle: War and diplomacy are inextricably linked, and it is as great a mistake to conduct diplomacy without considering military means as it is to wage war without diplomacy.

This truth has never enjoyed universal acceptance, but in modern times the conviction—or wish—that diplomacy can prevail without any connection to the use of force has become much more widespread. Many see war simply as the failure of diplomacy rather than its complement, and some argue that statesmen should not even consider using military power until they have exhausted all other means of achieving their aims. It is not only the evil of war that animates these critics, but the belief that force makes any kind of diplomacy all but impossible—that the angry "blowback" of elite and popular opinion in other nations necessarily overwhelms all diplomatic efforts, traditional or public, and outweighs any advantages that force may bring. "Hard" power and "soft" power, in other words, are mutually exclusive.

Choosing a Palatable Goal

Reality is more complex. As Kennan suggested nearly 60 years ago, when states act militarily without clearly defined political objectives supported by skillful diplomacy, they risk undermining their military successes by creating significant long-term problems. So, too, states that attempt to conduct complicated and dangerous diplomatic initiatives without the support of credible military options frequently fail to accomplish even their immediate goals—and sometimes create more severe long-term problems. The greatest danger lies neither in using force nor in avoiding it, but rather in failing to understand the intricate relationship between power and persuasion. Some rulers rely excessively upon the naked use of force, some upon unsupported diplomacy. History shows that the most successful of them skillfully integrate the two.

One of the keys to success in this endeavor lies in defining national ends that leaders and publics in other countries find at least minimally palatable. One can be an able diplomat and a talented commander on the battlefield, but even both abilities together will not bring success if they serve objectives that the rest of the world cannot tolerate. For the United States, there is no path that will spare it criticism and even outright opposition, but its broad goals of spreading freedom and political reform are ones that a great many people in the Muslim world and beyond will be able to accept. The challenge is not only to continue balancing power and persuasion but also simply to continue—to persist in the face of adversity and despite arguments that the very exercise of power ensures that the United States will never persuade and never prevail. . . .

Lessons of History

Today, those who are most reluctant to consider the use of force under any condition except in response to direct attack pin most of their hopes on the United Nations and other international organizations. In these forums, they believe, states should be able to peacefully resolve even their deepest differences. But history shows rather conclusively that the same principles that govern the affairs of nations also govern those of international organizations.

In 1923, for example, [Italian dictator] Benito Mussolini seized the Greek island of Corfu and demanded an exorbitant "reparation" from Athens after several Italian officials were assassinated in Greece. No evidence then or since has proven that Greeks were involved in the killings, and it is at least as likely that Mussolini's own agents were the culprits. The Greeks turned to the newly formed League of Nations.

Britain initially supported the Greeks' request, but it was virtually alone among the major powers. Prime Minister Stanley Baldwin's government had to choose: Forcing the issue into the League's purview would create a serious risk of war with Italy; giving in to Mussolini would destroy the League as an effective force in the post–Great War world order.

Baldwin found the task too daunting. Britain was war weary, and its forces were overextended and weakened by budget cuts (although it is clear in retrospect that the Italian navy could not have resisted the Royal Navy). In the end, the Greeks paid an indemnity they should not have owed, Mussolini abandoned an island he should never have occupied, and the case was taken away from the League of Nations. The precedent was thereby established for the Japanese invasion of Manchuria in 1931, to which the League made no response, and for the Italian invasion of Abyssinia in 1935, to which the League also had no meaningful reaction. The emasculation of the League in 1923 destroyed its credibility and virtually ensured its irrelevance in the major crises that lay ahead.

The Decisive Use of Force in Iraq

By contrast, the first Bush administration reacted to the Iraqi invasion of Kuwait in August 1990 in a manner designed not merely to resist Saddam Hussein's aggression but to strengthen

THE NEW ATLAS

the United Nations and prepare it for a central role in keeping the peace in the "new world order" after the Cold War. President George H. W. Bush quickly decided that he would use military force to reverse the Iraqi action. This was the critical decision. Although the task looked difficult at the time—Iraq had the fourth-largest military in the world, and early American casualty projections were as high as 50,000—the president believed that he had to act to prevent the immediate unraveling of the international order and to forestall legitimation of the principle that powerful states could use force to prevail in territorial disputes with their weaker neighbors.

Bush began a massive diplomatic effort to gain allies for the United States, win over world public opinion, and, above all, acquire clear and strong sanction from the UN for the operation to liberate Kuwait. The UN was galvanized by Bush's efforts. The discovery after the war that Saddam Hussein had been maintaining a vast weapons of mass destruction (WMD) program that had been virtually unknown to the principal international monitoring agencies led to a complete overhaul of those agencies, particularly the International Atomic Energy Agency (IAEA). Under its new director, Hans Blix, the IAEA and UNSCOM, the UN agency set up to oversee the destruction of Iraq's WMD program, pursued an increasingly successful effort in Iraq, supported periodically by the threat and use of U.S. airpower.

By the late 1990s, however, a growing American reluctance to use that power allowed the Iraqi dictator to eject UN inspectors. Saddam then began mothballing his WMD programs but was able to persuade the world that he still had them. The inspections effort in Iraq had been effective only when supported by the threat and occasional use of American military force.

Floundering in North Korea

The IAEA enjoyed no such support in North Korea. By 1994, Hans Blix had discovered a number of violations of the terms of the Nuclear Non-Proliferation Treaty, and the North Koreans had begun to interfere with the work of the inspectors in critical ways. At first, the [Bill] Clinton administration supported the IAEA in its struggle to force then-leader Kim Il Sung to come clean. As the crisis developed, however, the administration's concern over the danger from the North Korean army overwhelmed its desire to support the IAEA's efforts. The Clinton administration then brokered a deal with Kim Il Sung's son and successor, Kim Jong Il, that allowed North Korea to keep skirting the inspections program. As a result, the IAEA was unable to prevent the North Koreans from developing a nuclear weapon—and all indications are that they now possess one or two nuclear devices. Not surprisingly, recent negotiations, similarly unsupported by military force, have also failed to curb the North Korean nuclear program.

It may be that, in the end, as with Adolf Hitler and a few other die-hard aggressive leaders, there is no finding a peaceful solution with Kim Jong Il. Or it may be that some unforeseen change within North Korea will yield such an outcome.

It is certain, however, that diplomatic approaches unsupported by military power will not make much of an impression on Pyongyang, [North Korea's capital,] and that the continued failure to support international agencies charged with enforcing nonproliferation agreements will doom the cause of nonproliferation itself.

International organizations, especially those devoted to nonproliferation and peacekeeping, can succeed in difficult circumstances only when their efforts are supported by credible military means. Because such organizations help to identify current and future threats, and to galvanize international support behind the punishment of transgressors, the use of American power to support them is a good investment in long-term security.

Using Force to Ensure Peace

George Kennan was right: The existence of a powerful and battle-proven military makes the job of diplomats and political leaders vastly easier. However unhappy a defeated people may be with a given political settlement, or however resentful of military actions carried out against them, very few will take up arms again if convinced that they will again be defeated. Military half-measures designed to "send a message," such as those the [John F.] Kennedy and [Lyndon] Johnson administrations used in the early days of the Vietnam struggle, deceive no one and leave the door open for insurgent victory. Clearcut military triumph ... makes even the staunchest rebels more reluctant to try the test of battle again. The use of military force with any aim in mind other than victory is extremely dangerous and likely to be counterproductive.

Though the use of force may stir anger and resentment in an enemy population and damage a state's position in the world community, history suggests that both the animosity and the damage may be more fleeting than many suppose, and that their scale and duration may depend on many elements other than the mere fact that force was used. By far the most important element is the acceptability of the peace conditions imposed by the victor after the struggle. If the victor can devise terms that most of its foes and the rest of the international community can accept, then the animosity is likely to fade quickly. And if acceptable terms are coupled with continued military power, then the prospects for a lasting and stable peace are excellent.

The actions of the victorious state in the aftermath of the war are of great moment in determining the long-term consequences of military action. If the victor remains engaged with the defeated power in a positive way, helping to reintegrate it into an acceptable international system, and even to make good some of the damage done by the military operations, then memories of the pain inflicted by the war can be surprisingly short. The rise of a new and dangerous common enemy—which is not as unusual as one might suppose—can dramatically hasten this process.

Diplomacy is not the opposite of war, and war is not the failure of diplomacy. Both are tools required in various proportions in almost any serious foreign-policy situation. Yes, it is vitally important for the United States to "work with" and "support" international organizations, but their success in the foreseeable future will depend at least as much on the strength of the American military and on America's willingness to put its power behind those organizations. On that strength and on that willingness rests nothing less than the peace of the world.

> *"A militarized foreign policy offers Americans a country on a perpetual war footing, but not one that is more secure."*

U.S. Foreign Policy Should Focus on Diplomacy, Not Military Strength

Mel Goodman

In the following viewpoint Mel Goodman argues that American foreign policy is based on military strength and that the George W. Bush administration has proved it is willing to act unilaterally. Goodman maintains that this has upset relations with America's allies and engendered more hatred among its enemies. He suggests that the U.S. government should repair its image by participating in—not dominating—international peacemaking and security efforts. Only by pursuing diplomacy first, Goodman concludes, can the United States shed its imperial pretensions. Goodman is a senior fellow at the Center for International Policy in Washington, D.C.

Mel Goodman, "The Militarization of U.S. Foreign Policy," *Foreign Policy in Focus*, vol. 9, February 2004. Copyright © 2004 IRC and IPS. www.fpic.org. All rights reserved. Reproduced by permission.

As you read, consider the following questions:

1. In Goodman's view, why was the U.S. invasion of Iraq "rash and senseless"?

2. What nation does the author say may have imitated U.S. aggressiveness in dealing with its neighbor in 2003?

3. What, instead of war, does Goodman claim are the appropriate countermeasures to terrorism?

The fall of the Soviet Union handed the U.S. a unique opportunity, as the surviving superpower, to lead the world toward a period of greater cooperation and conflict resolution through the use of diplomacy, global organization, and international law. This great opportunity is being squandered, as the world becomes a more dangerous place. Military force is now looming larger than ever as the main instrument and organizing principle of U.S. foreign policy. In our new national security doctrine, in the shape of our federal budget, and in the missions of the agencies the budget funds, our government is being reshaped to weaken controls on its use of force and further incline our country toward war.

Force Should Be the Last Option

The U.S. decision to use force against Iraq was both rash and senseless, ignoring the fundamental premise that force should be the last, not the first, option. There was no near-term threat to the U.S. or to U.S. interests, let alone a clear and present danger. Yet Washington repeatedly passed up opportunities to use diplomacy or to build a coalition. Rather, it approached the problem assuming that, as the world's dominant military power, it had no need to gain the cooperation of the international community already organized to meet such challenges.

Since the 2000 election, and particularly in the wake of the Afghan War and the buildup to the invasion of Iraq, diplomacy has been shamefully abused. Rather than using international law to deal with suspected terrorists captured during the Afghan War, the U.S. opted for its own military tribunals and the suspension of accepted judicial procedures. It ignored such institutions as the United Nations International Court of Justice, which could have provided legal procedures based on international law. And it rejected established judicial civil procedures that guarantee the rights of the accused, including the representation by an attorney, a speedy trial, and access to evidence and witnesses for defense. In conducting a campaign of deceit to justify the invasion of Iraq, the [George W.] Bush administration created the greatest intelligence scandal in U.S. history.

With the invasion and occupation of Iraq, we have witnessed the end of the so-called post–cold war era and the escalation of a continuous, worldwide war on terrorism that has increased global insecurity. Nearly 150,000 American forces are occupying Iraq and Afghanistan, and the result is growing anarchy in both countries. President Bush has declared that the war against terrorism centers on Iraq. This has the ring of self-fulfilling prophecy, since Iraq had no terrorism problem [until] the U.S. invasion. A growing number at home and abroad are concerned Washington will resort to the use of preemptive force again, perhaps against other so-called "axis of evil" members, North Korea or Iran. . . .

Funding Military over Diplomacy

Reversing a trend that pre-dated the fall of the Soviet Union, the U.S. has increased its military budget to more than $400 billion and its intelligence budget to more than $40 billion. Current projections point to a defense budget of more than $500 billion before the end of the decade, with another $50 billion for the intelligence community. Led by Defense Secretary Donald Rumsfeld, the Department of Defense has moved aggressively to eclipse the State Department as the major locus of U.S. foreign policy, arrogating management of the intelligence community, and abandoning bipartisan policies of arms control and disarmament crafted over the past four decades. Funding cuts have prompted the Department of State to close consulates around the world and assign personnel of the well-funded CIA [Central Intelligence Agency] to diplomatic and consular posts. Though current defense costs represent nearly 20% of Washington's expenses, less than 1% of the federal budget is devoted to the needs of the State Department.

The misuse of sensitive information to justify the war against Iraq has precipitated the worst intelligence scandal in U.S. history, compromising the Bush administration's integrity. As former National Security Adviser Zbigniew Brzezinski argued, this intelligence failure has been "fueled by a demagogy that emphasizes worst-case scenarios, stimulates fear and induces a dichotomous view of world reality."

So instead of living in a new era of conciliation and conflict resolution, we are witnessing an ugly epilogue to the cold war that finds Washington acting alone instead of working with its traditional allies. It is important to understand how the U.S. was lured into this terrible cul-de-sac and how the nation should debate and adopt policies to reverse the Bush administration's dangerous neoconservative course.

Problems of Unilateral Action

U.S. foreign policy under the stewardship of Bush, [vice president Dick] Cheney, and Rumsfeld has been based on unilateralism and militarism. The condition of continuous, worldwide war has created an operational tempo for the military that the U.S. cannot afford and the Pentagon cannot endure. With so many "boots on the ground," the U.S. has triggered a series of diplomatic and political problems with both allies and adversaries. Moreover, the U.S. doctrine of preemptive war has set a dangerous precedent for other nations, validating the first Israeli attack against Syria in thirty years in October 2003 and perhaps justifying an Indian attack against Pakistan in the not-too-distant future. The radicalism of this doctrine is indicated by the spectrum of its opponents; in August 2002, for example, [former secretary of state] Henry Kissinger pointed out that "It is not in the American national interest to establish pre-emption as a universal principle available to every nation."

The major international problems that the U.S. faces today, particularly international terrorism and the proliferation of weapons of mass destruction (WMD) cannot be addressed unilaterally and cannot be resolved by the use of force. The same can be said for nontraditional security issues dealing with demographics, the environment, and AIDS. All of these problems require multilateral involvement and solutions.

What Needs to Be Done

In both Afghanistan and Iraq, nation-building and peacemaking must be internationalized under civilian—not military control—as quickly as possible. The Bush administration has commandeered more than half of America's ground forces to pacify Afghanistan and Iraq, and the U.S. is spending $5 billion a month in this effort with no end in sight. Neither the U.S. government nor the American people are prepared for the burdens of empire; U.S. military forces are overextended and are in no position to deal with emergencies that may arise, such as the genuine crisis on the Korean Peninsula.

The United Nations and non-government organizations (NGOs) must be involved far more extensively in order to share the burden of governance and elicit collective resources for the job of reconstruction. Many countries most experienced in the field of peacemaking are prepared to commit troops and treasure, but only if Washington is willing to yield its domination of the transition process. The U.S. must participate with both the UN and NATO [North Atlantic Treaty Organization] as group member—not hegemonic power. As

The U.S. Is Militarily Overcommitted

While the United States can militarily defeat just about any state in the world, without ongoing international cooperation we do not have the capacity to turn military victory into a stable peace or to fully remove the threat of terrorism. As the current phase of the Iraq War has demonstrated, the United States, despite spending almost as much as the rest of the world combined on its military, does not have sufficient forces to stabilize the situation on the ground without upsetting its standard rotation practices for active and reserve forces or drawing down its forces in other areas of potential conflict, such as the Korean Peninsula. The U.S. Army now has two-thirds of its 33 combat brigades deployed—16 in Iraq, two in Afghanistan, two in South Korea and one in the Balkans. In order to maintain a reasonable rotation policy, it should be deploying no more than half of its brigades at any one time.

Lawrence Korb, "Rumsfeld's Folly," American Prospect, November 2003.

Senator Chuck Hagel (R-NE) put it: "America needs more humility than hubris in the applications of American military power and the recognition that our interests are best served through alliances and consensus."

Diplomacy Must Be the First Option

International diplomacy, not military action, must be the first option in crisis management. The Bush administration has downplayed the role of international diplomacy in all crisis situations, including the Israeli-Palestinian peace process and the North Korean and Iranian nuclear challenges. In the Middle East, our aim should be the creation of a viable Palestinian state and security for Israel. This is probably best pursued by insisting that Israel abandon settlements in the occupied territories and by fostering Israeli acceptance of a Palestinian capital in East Jerusalem. The U.S. should also insist on an end to terrorism against Israelis, support of such a policy by members of the Arab League, and diplomatic recognition of Israel. In North Korea and Iran, the U.S. must establish or reestablish diplomatic relations, offer a combination of security guarantees and economic arrangements, and forge regional alignments to end the isolation of Pyongyang and Tehran. And Washington will need the cooperation of Iran and Syria to find a workable solution to the Iraqi crisis.

Intelligence and law enforcement must be the first options against terrorism; military force should be the last. West Europeans had to deal with terrorist organizations throughout the 1980s, and they did so effectively with law enforcement and intelligence agencies. Now that the terrorism problem is international, close relations with intelligence bodies are essential, as are knowledge of languages and regional studies in key areas. In the post-9/11 period, there have been no arrests or captures of key al Qaeda [terrorist organization] leaders that have not relied on liaison intelligence and support. Cooperation between law enforcement and intelligence agencies—not the application of unilateral force—is the key to success.

The U.S. must support arms control and disarmament in order to stop the proliferation of WMDs. The White House must preserve and enhance an effective arms control regime, not dismantle it. This means adhering to outstanding agreements, not abrogating treaties that previous administrations have signed. And it means desisting from actions that compromise agreements or open new areas for competition.

A militarized foreign policy offers Americans a country on a perpetual war footing, but not one that is more secure. The U.S. must return to the ABM [Anti-Ballistic Missile] Treaty, end the deployment of national missile defense, and abide by the Comprehensive Test Ban Treaty to end underground testing. U.S. support for arms control could end nuclear testing worldwide and even attract India and Pakistan to the Nuclear Nonproliferation Treaty. The current administration must commit itself to the agendas of Bush I [i.e., George H.W. Bush] and Bill Clinton to significantly reduce nuclear weapons and embrace international conventions on chemical and biological weapons. Washington must also end its development of low-yield nuclear weapons, such as bunker busters, and must prevent the weaponizing of outer space in order to return to the high moral ground in the quest for disarmament.

> "Withdrawal after a self-proclaimed 'victory' that leaves the insurgency largely intact and operational would fool no one."

Withdrawing the Military from Iraq Would Damage U.S. Credibility

Nikolas K. Gvosdev and Paul J. Saunders

In the following viewpoint Nikolas K. Gvosdev and Paul J. Saunders contend that the U.S. military must succeed in Iraq or America's global credibility will suffer. To withdraw the army before Iraq is stabilized might signify to the world that the overthrowing of Saddam Hussein's regime was reckless and motivated by self-interested imperialism. To avoid this, the authors suggest that the U.S. military should not be squandered policing Iraq; instead it should be given the objective of destroying the terrorist forces that continue to make Iraq a battleground. In that way, the military's mission would be clear-cut, and the U.S. government could allow the Iraqis more authority in rebuilding their own state. Gvosdev is editor of the National Interest. *Saunders is executive director of the Nixon Center and a contributing editor to the* National Interest.*

Nikolas K. Gvosdev and Paul J. Saunders, "Defining Victory," *National Interest*, vol. 81, fall 2005, pp. 5-7. Copyright © *The National Interest* 2005, Washington D.C. Reproduced by permission.

As you read, consider the following questions:

1. According to the authors, what problems would arise if America withdrew prematurely from Iraq?

2. In Gvosdev and Saunders's view, what would be the risks of an "unlimited commitment" in Iraq?

3. Who do the authors believe should be given the task of providing internal security for Iraq?

America has no choice but to succeed in Iraq. The country's collapse could fuel chaos in the Middle East; a terrorist base there could support new attacks in America, in the region, in Europe and worldwide. The consequences of defeat in Iraq extend beyond this as well. As the only global superpower, the United States can afford to make mistakes—even big ones. But it cannot allow itself to be defeated in a priority-defining project like Iraq. After investing the lives and well-being of American soldiers, $200 billion in taxpayer funds and substantial amounts of international political capital, failure could be very damaging both abroad and at home.

Why and how we got into Iraq and what choices could have been made differently: This is not central to when and how we get out. Only victory is. This is not to say that the [George W.] Bush Administration has not made mistakes in the war and in the occupation. The U.S. assessment, shared by other governments, that Iraq was energetically engaged in WMD [weapons of mass destruction] programs was clearly incorrect. The administration's expectations for postwar Iraq were also incorrect and led to a series of decisions—like disbanding the Iraqi army and other state institutions with little thought given to what would replace them—that have made it harder rather than easier to set Iraq back on its feet. The role of [Iraqi deputy prime minister] Ahmed Chalabi and company in shaping U.S. policy certainly deserves much greater scrutiny in this connection. But the appropriate study and debate of "lessons learned" should not crowd out discussion of the way forward.

Unfortunately, at the political level that discussion has been weak so far. In fairness, the war in Iraq is a problem with no good solution. Still, after two years (and with no end in sight), we believe it's time for hard thinking.

The Perils of Claiming an Early Victory

Some—Republicans and Democrats both—are calling for the administration to develop an exit strategy and to implement a schedule for the withdrawal of American forces by a designated date, "limited only by steps to ensure the safety" of U.S. troops, in the words of the so-called "Homeward Bound" legislation. Others, who see Iraq as an instrument to spread freedom and transform the Middle East, seem prepared to accept a virtually indefinite commitment of American forces, resources and attention.

Both strategies are problematic. Withdrawal after a self-proclaimed "victory" that leaves the insurgency largely intact and operational would fool no one; Americans and others around the world know a real victory when they see one—and they know a defeat when they smell it. Setting aside the fact that it would allow a cancerous terrorism problem to metastasize, withdrawal would lead to inevitable (if inaccurate) comparisons to the U.S. defeat in Vietnam, intensified speculation about "imperial overstretch" and declining American power, and a costly loss of credibility and influence.

The reality is that to be effective in the international system, the United States must be respected by the good and feared by the evil. Recklessness in foreign policy decision-making can lead the good to fear rather than respect us—and encourage efforts to limit U.S. power—while fecklessness produces neither respect nor fear but contempt. Many outside the United States might interpret withdrawal from Iraq without a clear victory as a feckless end to what they saw as a reckless war and would draw appropriate conclusions. As [terrorism analyst] Alexis Debat outlined in the Summer 2005 issue of the *National Interest*, it would also allow international jihadists [Islamic extremists] to consolidate a "new base in Iraq around which the technical, financial and human resources of Jihad, Inc., can again coalesce."

Saying that U.S. forces will stay in Iraq as long as they are needed and not one day longer is not really an answer. Nor is saying that we will leave when the Iraqis can "take care of themselves." These statements are very difficult to define in operational terms; they also run the risk of encouraging Iraqi free-riding, limiting the pressure on Iraqi political leaders and citizens to make tough decisions.

President Bush is correct not to give the impression that U.S. determination to achieve a successful outcome in Iraq is wavering. But unwavering determination and its implicit or even explicit willingness to "pay any price" are not sufficient alone as a policy. In fact, in combination with expansive neo-Wilsonian goals [i.e., similar to U.S. president Woodrow Wilson's], an unlimited commitment can lead to a quagmire, burdening the United States with unbearable costs and an un-acceptable distraction from pressing international problems like Iran and North Korea and longer-term challenges like the rise of China. The United States is not omnipotent. Our financial resources are limited; the time and attention of our leaders is limited; the capacity of our institutions (including the White House staff, the military, the intelligence agencies and the State Department) is limited; and our political capital with other governments is limited. Fortunately, with an appropriate definition of U.S. objectives, it is still possible to achieve a realistic victory in Iraq.

What do we mean by "realistic victory"? We mean a meaningful success that would be widely interpreted as a victory by traditional international standards, namely, destroying a hostile regime and establishing a reasonably friendly and non-tyrannical government that threatens neither the United States nor regional allies like Israel.

The Military Should Concentrate on Destroying Terrorists

Of course, because of some of the overblown rhetoric about Iraq, some will argue that anything short of full Jeffersonian democracy along the Tigris and Euphrates [rivers] is a failure. We see no reason to indulge such fantasies. Democracy according to the standards of Western post-industrial states is not a precondition for victory; nor, as the London [transit system] bombings tragically illustrated, is it a panacea for the problem of terrorism, whether homegrown or internationally inspired. Minimal standards of pluralism are all that is required to undermine most domestic support for terror—and they largely exist in Iraq. Paraphrasing Winston Churchill's famous statement about democracy, what Iraq already has may not be perfect, but it's better than the alternatives.

Rather than attempting to micromanage Iraqi politics and engineer the government and constitution, the United States should concentrate on destroying the international terrorists who have flocked to Iraq and preventing them from turning the country into a base. This approach would allow for a considerably reduced military presence (especially among politically sensitive National Guard and reserve units) even before more Iraqi forces are trained and deployed, with U.S. forces based outside cities and dedicated to securing Iraq's porous borders and fighting the terrorists and "dead-enders." Let the Iraqis take over responsibility for security in the cities so as to reduce our visibility and vulnerability there—and let Iraqis decide on the best means to combat internal threats to their security. (At a minimum, this should further encourage the Shi'a-dominated government to reach out to and accommodate Sunni leaders.) To the extent that U.S. forces play an active role in urban operations, it should be clear that when we act, we are acting in partnership with the Iraqi government and not unilaterally. As Robert Tucker and David Hendrickson note in their contribution to [the fall 2005 issue of the

No More Vietnams

When conservatives repossess the motto "No more Vietnams," it will be a perfect occasion to address one of the most important questions of our time. Is American policy based on rights or on duties? Is America in Iraq because of our duties or their rights? If "their rights" is the answer, liberals are correct: We have stuck our necks out unnecessarily; we could just as easily have let someone else worry about it, the way France and Germany did. If the answer is "our duties," we had no choice. We had an obligation to take charge of our own safety in a world that is lousy with terrorists, and we had to face up to our obligations as the world's strongest nation. And obviously we have duties in nations besides Iraq also. America doesn't have the power to help everybody—which is no excuse for helping nobody.

American character is on the line. For the sake of this nation—of its good name, its big heart, the sacrifices of its many brave defenders, the genius of its creators—of its greatness, in short—conservatives had better not lose this fight.

The administration was wrong to let Americans get the idea that Iraq would be easy. But it was right to fight. And because Iraq is exactly Vietnam all over again, our eventual victory won't only be good for Iraq, the Middle East, and peace on earth. It will repair American self-respect.

David Gelernter, "No More Vietnams; This Time, Let's Finish the Job," Weekly Standard, May 8, 2006.

National Interest], that has not been the case in the past, and this in turn has helped to stir up ill will against coalition forces.

More broadly, success requires giving real incentives to ordinary Iraqis. Let's face it: To quote Thomas Paine, Iraqis are going to be summer soldiers and sunshine patriots. Giving the Iraqi government clear responsibility for domestic security—the next logical step in establishing full sovereignty and something Iraq's government naturally seems to want—could change the way many Iraqis think about their country.

Focusing on the Right Goals

We are under no illusions that there is any cheap or quick solution to Iraq two years on. The strategy we propose is not a simple one to pursue, especially as terrorist attacks in Iraq focus increasingly on provoking sectarian conflict in an apparent effort to generate more violence or even civil war. The temptation to believe that we are more knowledgeable and effective in resolving internal Iraqi disagreements than the Iraqis themselves will be considerable, especially in the wake of the inevitable further setbacks that remain ahead. But the Iraqis must solve their own problems, and waiting until they are "ready" when attacks average 65 per day means waiting indefinitely.

We hope that Iraq will eventually become a liberal democracy with strong checks and balances, firm protections for women and minorities, and other hallmarks of free societies. But achieving all this could take some time, and trying to do too much too soon could distract us from achieving what is genuinely essential: depriving Al-Qaeda of a base, closing Iraq's borders to foreign fighters, and developing a central government that is capable of ensuring some degree of stability without repressive methods or becoming too close to Iran, or both. As America's involvement in Iraq has already demonstrated, these goals alone are a tall order. They are also pursued more effectively by a smaller, less visible, less provocative military presence than is required for an ambitious nation-building project to create a beacon for the Middle East.

It is encouraging that the Bush Administration appears to be moving toward a significant withdrawal of forces from

Iraq. Yet it is essential that this or any withdrawal be accompanied by a recalibration of our goals and strategy.

The United States can achieve a realistic victory in Iraq without killing every last insurgent, capturing every Al-Qaeda recruit, ironing out every dispute between Arabs and Kurds, Sunnis and Shi'as, secularists and Islamists, or solving every other thorny political or constitutional problem. Americans and others will recognize victory if we have managed to break the back of Al-Qaeda in Iraq and left in place an Iraqi government committed and able to prevent the jihadists from returning. Then the United States can turn its attention to other pressing problems that threaten the peace and prosperity of the Republic.

| "A rapid reversal of our present course in Iraq would improve U.S. credibility around the world."

Withdrawing the Military from Iraq Would Improve U.S. Credibility

William E. Odom

Lieutenant General William E. Odom (retired) is a senior fellow at the Hudson Institute and a professor at Yale University. In the following viewpoint he rebuts many common arguments used to support continued U.S. military occupation of Iraq. According to Odom, U.S. forces in Iraq are already caught in a quagmire that has damaged America's global reputation. Pulling out of Iraq is the only means to repair that damage because it would show critics that America is strong enough to admit its mistakes. Furthermore, freeing the nation from the Iraq nightmare would allow the U.S. government, in Odom's phrasing, to "regain diplomatic and military mobility."

As you read, consider the following questions:

1. Why does Odom contend that Iraq will never be a liberal democracy friendly to the United States?

William E. Odom, "Cut and Run? You Bet. Why America Must Get Out of Iraq Now," *Foreign Policy*, vol. 154, May-June 2006, pp. 60-61. Copyright 2006 Carnegie Endowment for International Peace. Reproduced by permission.

2. According to the author, how has the U.S. invasion of Iraq encouraged terrorism?

3. In Odom's view, how will a U.S. withdrawal from Iraq possibly help bring stability to Iraq and solutions to larger problems in the Middle East?

Withdraw immediately or stay the present course? That is the key question about the war in Iraq today. American public opinion is now decidedly against the war. From liberal New England, where citizens pass town-hall resolutions calling for withdrawal, to the conservative South and West, where more than half of "red state" citizens oppose the war, Americans want out. That sentiment is understandable.

The prewar dream of a liberal Iraqi democracy friendly to the United States is no longer credible. No Iraqi leader with enough power and legitimacy to control the country will be pro-American. Still, U.S. President George W. Bush says the United States must stay the course. Why? Let's consider his administration's most popular arguments for not leaving Iraq.

Will Withdrawal Encourage Civil War and Terrorism?

If we leave, there will be a civil war. In reality, a civil war in Iraq began just weeks after U.S. forces toppled Saddam. Any close observer could see that then; today, only the blind deny it. Even President Bush, who is normally impervious to uncomfortable facts, recently admitted that Iraq has peered into the abyss of civil war. He ought to look a little closer. Iraqis are fighting Iraqis. Insurgents have killed far more Iraqis than Americans. That's civil war.

Withdrawal will encourage the terrorists. True, but that is the price we are doomed to pay. Our continued occupation of Iraq also encourages the killers—precisely because our invasion made Iraq safe for them. Our occupation also left the surviving Baathists [Saddam Hussein's ruling party in Iraq] with one choice: Surrender, or ally with al Qaeda [the terrorist organization responsible for the September 11, 2001, attacks upon America]. They chose the latter. Staying the course will not change this fact. Pulling out will most likely result in Sunni groups' turning against al Qaeda and its sympathizers, driving them out of Iraq entirely.

Before U.S. forces stand down, Iraqi security forces must stand up. The problem in Iraq is not military competency; it is political consolidation. Iraq has a large officer corps with plenty of combat experience from the Iran-Iraq war. Moktada al-Sadr's Shiite militia fights well today without U.S. advisors, as do Kurdish pesh merga [guerrilla] units. The problem is loyalty. To whom can officers and troops afford to give their loyalty? The political camps in Iraq are still shifting. So every Iraqi soldier and officer today risks choosing the wrong side. As a result, most choose to retain as much latitude as possible to switch allegiances. All the U.S. military trainers in the world cannot remove that reality. But political consolidation will. It should by now be clear that political power can only be established via Iraqi guns and civil war, not through elections or U.S. colonialism by ventriloquism.

Will Withdrawal Damage U.S. Morale and Credibility?

Setting a withdrawal deadline will damage the morale of U.S. troops. Hiding behind the argument of troop morale shows no willingness to accept the responsibilities of command. The truth is, most wars would stop early if soldiers had the choice of whether or not to continue. This is certainly true in Iraq, where a withdrawal is likely to raise morale among U.S. forces. A recent Zogby poll suggests that most U.S. troops would welcome an early withdrawal deadline. But the strategic question of how to extract the United States from the Iraq disaster is not a matter to be decided by soldiers. [German military strategist] Carl von Clausewitz spoke of two kinds of courage:

"How do you think the war with Iraq is affecting the United States' image in the world? Is the war making the U.S. image in the world better, making it worse, or is the war having no effect on the U.S. image in the world?"

Better	Worse	No Effect	Unsure
10%	72%	12%	6%

"Do you think the U.S. presence in Iraq is leading to greater stability in the Middle East, less stability, or doesn't it have any effect on the stability of the Middle East?"

Greater Stability	Less Stability	No Effect	Unsure
25%	41%	25%	9%

"Do you think the war with Iraq has made U.S. diplomatic efforts in the rest of the Middle East easier, harder, or has it had no effect?"

Easier	Harder	No Effect	Unsure
10%	69%	16%	5%

"If the U.S. stays in Iraq for several more years, do you think that will eventually make the United States more safe from terrorism, less safe, or won't it make any difference?"

More Safe	Less Safe	No Difference	Unsure
27%	21%	50%	2%

"Do you think the United States should or should not set a timetable for the withdrawal of U.S. troops from Iraq?"

Should	Should Not	Unsure
56%	40%	4%

SOURCE: CBS News/*New York Times* poll, July 21–25, 2006.

first, bravery in the face of mortal danger; second, the willingness to accept personal responsibility for command decisions. The former is expected of the troops. The latter must be demanded of high-level commanders, including the president.

Withdrawal would undermine U.S. credibility in the world. Were the United States a middling power, this case might hold some water. But for the world's only superpower, it's patently phony. A rapid reversal of our present course in Iraq would improve U.S. credibility around the world. The same argument was made against withdrawal from Vietnam. It was proved wrong then and it would be proved wrong today. Since Sept. 11, 2001, the world's opinion of the United States has plummeted, with the largest short-term drop in American history. The United States now garners as much international esteem as Russia. Withdrawing and admitting our mistake would reverse this trend. Very few countries have that kind of corrective capacity. I served as a military attaché in the U.S. Embassy in Moscow during Richard Nixon's Watergate crisis. When Nixon resigned, several Soviet officials who had previously expressed disdain for the United States told me they were astonished. One diplomat said, "Only your country is powerful enough to do this. It would destroy my country."

Now Is the Time to Leave Iraq

Two facts, however painful, must be recognized, or we will remain perilously confused in Iraq. First, invading Iraq was not in the interests of the United States. It was in the interests of Iran and al Qaeda. For Iran, it avenged a grudge against Saddam for his invasion of the country in 1980. For al Qaeda, it made it easier to kill Americans. Second, the war has paralyzed the United States in the world diplomatically and strategically. Although relations with Europe show signs of marginal improvement, the trans-Atlantic alliance still may not survive the war. Only with a rapid withdrawal from Iraq will Washington regain diplomatic and military mobility. Tied down like Gulliver in the sands of Mesopotamia, we simply cannot attract the diplomatic and military cooperation necessary to win the real battle against terror. Getting out of Iraq is the precondition for any improvement.

In fact, getting out now may be our only chance to set things right in Iraq. For starters, if we withdraw, European politicians would be more likely to cooperate with us in a strategy for stabilizing the greater Middle East. Following a withdrawal, all the countries bordering Iraq would likely respond favorably to an offer to help stabilize the situation. The most important of these would be Iran. It dislikes al Qaeda as much as we do. It wants regional stability as much as we do.

It wants to produce more oil and gas and sell it. If its leaders really want nuclear weapons, we cannot stop them. But we can engage them.

None of these prospects is possible unless we stop moving deeper into the "big sandy" of Iraq. America must withdraw now.

> *"Unless [the Iranians] are stopped or significantly delayed by military actions, they will become a nuclear power within a few years."*

The United States Should Attack Iran

Alan Dershowitz

In the following viewpoint Alan Dershowitz, a law professor at Harvard University, states that Iran is close to developing nuclear weapons and, as a result, will likely threaten peace in the Middle East. Dershowitz argues that the United States should use preemptive military action to remove the threat, but he acknowledges that American forces are already tied down in the ongoing conflict in Iraq. In hindsight, given the fact that the United States chose to target Iraq instead of Iran, Dershowitz believes the opportunity to effectively eliminate the more radical and destabilizing force in the region has now been lost.

As you read, consider the following questions:

1. In Dershowitz's view, what has been Iran's response to the George W. Bush administration's "loud barking" about mounting a credible strike against Iran?

Alan Dershowitz, "We Should Attack Iran—but We Can't," *Spectator*, April 22, 2006. Copyright © 2006 by *The Spectator*. Reproduced by permission of *The Spectator*.

2. According to the author, what are the three reasons that Iran's regime does not fear a preemptive attack from Israel?

3. For what two reasons would a nuclear-armed Iraq be, in Dershowitz's opinion, "the most dangerous nation in the world"?

Face it. Iran will get the bomb. It has already test-fired rockets capable of targeting the entire Middle East and much of southern Europe. And it claims to have 40,000 suicide volunteers eager to deploy terrorism—even nuclear terrorism—against its enemies. With a nuclear capacity, the Islamic Republic of Iran will instantly achieve the status of superpower to which Iraq aspired.

Nothing will deter Iran. Sanctions are paper protests to an oil-rich nation. Diplomacy has already failed because Russia and China are playing both sides. Sabotage, bribery—even assassination of nuclear scientists—may delay but will not prevent Iran from becoming a nuclear power. That leaves military threats and, ultimately, military action.

Threats Are Not Working

First, consider military threats. They are already coming from two sources: the US and Israel. Neither is working, for very different reasons.

The Iranians would probably give up their nuclear weapons programme if their leaders truly believed that refusal to do so would produce an Iraq-like attack—an all-out invasion, regime change and occupation. Leaders, even religious leaders, fear imprisonment and death. Only the United States is capable of mounting such a sustained attack.

But the continuing war in Iraq has made it impossible for the US to mount a credible threat, because American public opinion would not accept a second war—or so the Iranians

Iran Will Not Bow to Diplomatic Pressure

A military option against Iran's nuclear facilities is feasible. A diplomatic solution to the nuclear crisis is preferable, but without a credible military option and the will to implement it, diplomacy will not succeed. The announcement of uranium enrichment [in April 2006] by President Mahmoud Ahmadinejad shows Iran will not bow easily to diplomatic pressure. The existence of a military option may be the only means of persuading Iran—the world's leading sponsor of terrorism—to back down from producing nuclear weapons.

Thomas McInerney, "Target: Iran; Yes, There Is a Feasible Military Option Against the Mullahs' Nuclear Program," Weekly Standard, April 24, 2006.

believe. Moreover, America's allies in the war against Iraq—most particularly Great Britain—would not support an attack on Iran.

That is precisely why the Bush administration is barking so loudly. It wants to convince the Iranian leadership that it is preparing to bite—to attack, invade and destroy their regime, perhaps even with the use of tactical nuclear weapons. But it's not working. It is only causing the Iranian leaders themselves to bark louder; to exaggerate their progress towards completing a nuclear weapon and to threaten terrorist retaliation by its suicide volunteers if Iran were to be attacked.

The war in Iraq is a two-edged sword when it comes to Iran. One edge demonstrates that the US is willing and able to topple dictatorial regimes which it regards as dangerous. That is the edge the Bush administration is trying to showcase. The other edge represents the failure of Iraq—widespread public distrust of intelligence claims, fear of becoming bogged down in another endless war, strident opposition at home and abroad. That is the edge being seen by the Iranian leaders. The US threat is seen as hollow.

War with Israel

That leaves the Israeli threat, which is real, but limited. Who could blame Israel for seeking to destroy the emerging nuclear capacity of an enemy nation whose leader, as recently as 14 April 2006, threatened to eliminate 'the Zionist regime' by 'one storm'—a clear reference to a nuclear attack. His predecessor, the more moderate Hashemi Rafsanjani 'speculated [in 2001] that in a nuclear exchange with Israel his country might lose 15 million people, which would amount to a small "sacrifice" from among the one billion Muslims worldwide in exchange for the lives of five million Israeli Jews'. According to the journalist who interviewed him, 'he seemed pleased with his formulation'.

These threats of a nuclear attack are being taken seriously by Israeli leaders, even if they are neither imminent nor certain. Israelis remember apocalyptic threats from an earlier dictator that were not taken seriously. This time those threatened have the military capacity to confront the danger and are likely to do so if it becomes more likely. Even if Israelis believe there is only a 5 per cent chance that Iran would attack Israel with nuclear weapons, the risk of national annihilation would be too great for any nation—and most especially one built on the ashes of the Holocaust—to ignore.

The Iranian leaders understand this. They take seriously the statements made by Israeli leaders that they will never accept a nuclear Iran under its present leadership. They fully expect an attack from Israel when they come close to producing a nuclear weapon. Why then are they not deterred by the realistic prospect of an Israeli pre-emptive (or preventive) strike? For three related reasons. First, an Israeli attack would be a limited, surgical strike (or series of strikes). It would not be accompanied by a full-scale invasion, occupation and regime change.

Second, it would only delay production of a nuclear bomb, because it would be incomplete. Some nuclear facilities would be missed or only damaged, because they are 'hardened' and/or located in populated areas. The third and most important reason is that an attack by Israel would solidify the Iranian regime. It would make Iran into the victim of 'Zionist aggression' and unify Muslims, both inside and outside of Iran, against their common enemies. I say enemies because regardless of what role the US played or did not play in an Israeli attack, the US would share the blame in the radical Islamic world.

I am not going so far as to argue that the Iranian leadership would welcome an Israeli attack, but it would quickly turn such an attack to its advantage. If matters get worse domestically for the Iranian regime—if the nascent anti-Ahmadinejad 'democratic' or 'secular' movements were to strengthen—Ahmadinejad might actually get to the point of welcoming, even provoking or faking, an attack from Israel. This is why the threat from Israel will not work as a deterrent.

America Fought the Wrong War

So we have two threats: one from a superpower—the US—that can but won't bring about regime change. The other from a regional power—Israel—that may well attack but, if it does, will not only fail to produce regime change, but may actually strengthen the existing regime.

The Iranians will persist therefore in their efforts to secure nuclear weapons. Unless they are stopped or significantly delayed by military actions, they will become a nuclear power within a few years—precisely how many is unknown and probably unknowable.

Armed with nuclear weapons and ruled by religious fanatics, Iran will become the most dangerous nation in the world. There is a small but still real possibility that it could initiate a suicidal nuclear exchange with Israel. There is a far greater likelihood that it could hand over nuclear material to one of its terrorist surrogates or that some rogue elements could steal nuclear material. This would pose a direct threat to the United States and all its allies.

The world should not accept these risks if there are reasonable steps available to prevent or reduce them. The question remains: are any such steps feasible? Probably not, as long as the US remains bogged down in Iraq. History may well conclude that America and Britain fought the wrong preventive war against a country that posed no real threat, and that fighting that wrong war stopped them fighting the right preventive war against a country that did pose a danger to world peace.

Though the doctrine of preventive war is easily abused—as it was in Iraq—sometimes it is a necessary evil. The failure of Britain and France to wage a preventive war against Nazi Germany in the mid-1930s cost the world millions of lives. Will the same be said some day about the failure to prevent Iran from developing nuclear weapons?

| "Military action might at best suppress
Iran's nuclear ambitions temporarily."

The United States Should Not Attack Iran

Richard K. Betts

In the following viewpoint Richard K. Betts argues that the United States must choose an alternative to military action to counter Iran's efforts to develop nuclear weapons. Air strikes, Betts says, would be too ineffective to halt the Iranian program, and a full-scale invasion is impossible because of U.S. troop commitments in Iraq. Betts suggests that diplomatic and economic pressures are the best hope for keeping Iran from pursuing its nuclear agenda. Richard K. Betts is the director of the Saltzman Institute of War and Peace Studies at Columbia University in New York.

As you read, consider the following questions:

1. According to Betts, what lessons should the United States learn from the air strikes it made against Iraq's nuclear facilities?

Richard K. Betts, "The Osirak Fallacy," *National Interest*, vol. 83, Spring 2006, pp. 22-25. Copyright © *The National Interest* 2006, Washington D.C. Reproduced by permission.

2. What does the author mean when he describes efforts to halt nuclear proliferation as "ultimately a rear-guard action"?

3. How would a containment and deterrence strategy work, in Betts's view?

As pressure mounts to reckon with Iran's nascent nuclear program, some strategists are arguing that the United States has run out of alternatives to military action. Many of them are pointing to Israel's 1981 air attack on Iraq's Osirak reactor as a model for action—a bold stroke flying in the face of all international opinion that nipped Iraq's nuclear capability in the bud or at least postponed a day of reckoning. This reflects widespread misunderstanding of what that strike accomplished. Contrary to prevalent mythology, there is no evidence that Israel's destruction of Osirak delayed Iraq's nuclear weapons program. The attack may actually have accelerated it.

Osirak is not applicable to Iran anyway, since an air strike on a single reactor is not a model for the comprehensive campaign that would be required to deal, even unsatisfactorily, with the extensive, concealed and protected program that Iran is probably developing. As the United States crafts nonproliferation policy, it should soberly consider the actual effect of the Osirak attack and the limitations of even stronger air action.

In contrast to a ground war, air power has the allure of quick, clean, decisive action without messy entanglement. Smash today, gone tomorrow. Iraq's nuclear program demonstrates how unsuccessful air strikes can be even when undertaken on a massive scale. Recall the surprising discoveries after the [first] Iraq War. In 1991 coalition air forces destroyed the known nuclear installations in Iraq, but when UN inspectors went into the country after the war, they unearthed a huge infrastructure for nuclear weapons development that had been completely unknown to Western intelligence before the war.

Comparing Iraq and Iran

Obliterating the Osirak reactor did not put the brakes on Saddam's nuclear weapons program because the reactor that was destroyed could not have produced a bomb on its own and was not even necessary for producing a bomb. Nine years after Israel's attack on Osirak, Iraq was very close to producing a nuclear weapon. Had Saddam been smart enough in 1990 to wait a year longer, he might have been able to have a nuclear weapon in his holster when he invaded Kuwait. . . .

Iraq's Osirak-era capabilities were not remotely comparable to Iran's current nuclear program, which is far more advanced. Today's Iran has also been on notice for a long time that it is in the crosshairs of American military planners. It would be surprising if strategists in Tehran [Iran's capital] have failed to disperse and conceal important facilities in the interests of frustrating U.S. intelligence collection. An American air campaign could easily destroy all identified or suspected nuclear facilities—at least any not located in very deeply buried bunkers—but attack planners could not be sure that all crucial facilities had been hit, because they could not be confident that all had been found.

Desperation or bravado has led some strategists to question that reality. While they recognize that an air campaign would not guarantee full destruction of Iran's nuclear capability or even prevent Iran from rebuilding, they reason that it could at least delay the program. The question remains, then, would a strike that was successful in wiping out a big chunk of Iran's program be more effective than Israel's venture in 1981?

With more to destroy than in Iraq back then, the evolving Iranian program might be more disrupted, but by the same token more hidden capabilities might survive. When it comes to nuclear weapons, the key is not how much capability a preventive attack eliminates, but how much it does not. Unless

Three Reasons Not to Attack Iran

One excellent reason not to move forthwith to bomb Iran's nuclear installations . . . [is that] Iranians are our once and future allies. Except for a narrow segment of extremists, they do not view themselves as enemies of the United States, but rather as the exact opposite: at a time when Americans are unpopular in all other Muslim countries, most Iranians become distinctly more friendly when they learn that a visitor is American. They must not be made to feel that they were attacked by the very country they most admire, where so many of their own relatives and friends have so greatly prospered, and with which they wish to restore the best of relations.

There is a second good reason not to act precipitously. In essence, we should not bomb Iran because the worst of its leaders positively want to be bombed—and are doing their level best to bring that about. . . . In a transparent political maneuver, [Iranian president Mahmoud] Ahmadinejad tries to elicit nationalist support at home by provoking hostile reactions abroad, through his calls for the destruction of Israel, his clumsy version of Holocaust denial that is plainly an embarrassment even to other extremists, and, above all, his repeated declarations that Iran is about to repudiate the Non-Proliferation Treaty it ratified in 1970.

There is a third reason, too. The effort to build nuclear weapons started more than three decades ago, yet the regime is still years away from producing a bomb.

Edward N. Luttwak, "*Three Reasons Not to Bomb Iran—Yet*," Commentary, *May 2006.*

the Iranians have been extremely negligent, they have not left all of their enrichment capacity in locations accessible to American intelligence collectors and Air Force targeters. . . .

The Consequences of Military Action

Political, diplomatic and military obstacles to taking action in Iran have been well recognized. Strategists who think of themselves as stalwart, steely-eyed and far-seeing regard these obstacles as challenges to be simply overcome or disregarded in order to do what is necessary, even if it is less than a perfect solution. But if bombing known nuclear sites were to mean that Tehran could only produce a dozen weapons in 15 years rather than, say, two dozen in ten years, would the value of the delay outweigh the high costs? The costs would not be just political and diplomatic, but strategic as well. Provoking further alienation of non-Western governments and Islamic populations around the world would undermine the global War on Terror. Inflaming Iranian nationalism would turn a populace that is currently divided in its attitudes toward the West into a united front against the United States. Rage within Tehran's government would probably trigger retaliation via more state-sponsored terrorist actions by [extremist group] Hizballah or other Iranian agents.

The military option that is possible would be ineffective, while the one that would be effective is not possible. The military action that would work—an invasion of Iran—cannot be done, since America's volunteer army has already reached the breaking point in handling missions less challenging than subduing Iran would be. The only means of definitively preventing Iran from acquiring nuclear weapons would be occupying the country forever. . . .

What else should Washington do? There is no good answer. The crusade to keep all second-rate powers from acquiring a nuclear weapon—which, we should remember, is now sixty-year-old technology—can succeed in some cases for some time, but it is ultimately a rear-guard action. Regarding both Iran and North Korea—which is probably more dangerous than Iran yet somehow has slipped into second place in proclamations of alarm—the two answers may be unsatisfactory but are less unsatisfactory than other conceivable options.

Political and Economic Inducements

One answer is the prosaic, two-track strategy of political and economic carrots and sticks. Tehran should be offered diplomatic concessions if it comes back into full compliance with requirements of the Nuclear Non-Proliferation Treaty (NPT), including the more intrusive inspections mandated under the Additional Protocol. Concessions would be a difficult choice, since they would compromise the War on Terror, given Iran's bad record as a state sponsor. But limiting the nuclear threat is a higher priority.

It is also true that this approach is no foolproof guarantee of non-proliferation. Iran could presumably cheat and maintain clandestine weapon-development programs. Still, it would provide the only incentive for Iranian restraint, and inspections would at least complicate and impede concealment of illicit activity.

If, on the other hand, Tehran fully disengages from the obligations of the NPT, the United States should promote multilateral tightening and extension of economic sanctions. Unfortunately, the self-inflicted wound of the invasion of Iraq poisoned the well for convincing fence-sitters in other countries to sign on to such measures. America's credibility regarding the threat posed by Iran has been weakened by its unsubstantiated claims of Iraq's weapons of mass destruction.

Containment Strategy

The second component—which is unsatisfactory but better than the alternatives—is to replicate the Cold War strategy of containment and deterrence until such time that the regime in Tehran mellows or is replaced from within. Many today forget that [Joseph] Stalin's Soviet Union [USSR] and Mao Zedong's China were seen as more threatening in both capabilities and intentions than are today's mullahs in Tehran. For reasons remarkably similar to those proclaimed today, alarmed American strategists discussed the option of preventive war against the USSR in the 1950s and against China in the 1960s. Fortunately, the U.S. government rejected those ideas. Then as now, it was risky to tilt towards the hope that steady defensive resistance—rather than aggressive military action—would hold the line until enemies eventually reformed or stood down. Now as then, that risk is uncomfortable but remains the best among bad options.

To some in the [George W.] Bush Administration, this reasoning smacks of defeatism. Which way will the president tilt? Will the born politician in George Bush guess that another military adventure in the midst of the Iraq fiasco would devastate his standing, given that he is already on the ropes; or will the born-again crusader in Bush wager on bold and decisive use of American muscle, in the belief it would restore public confidence?

Neoconservative zealotry has fallen from grace in the second Bush Administration, and a prudent State Department has risen in influence under [secretary of state] Condoleezza Rice. Still, the rationale for military action could appeal to some of the stalwart staffers around Bush, [vice president Dick] Cheney and [former secretary of defense Donald] Rumsfeld. Many of these men's faith in force was annealed in the crucible of September 11 and remains unshaken by the Iraq experience. They confuse caution as a cover for timidity and believe that disregarding liberal conventional wisdom is a mark of Churchillian courage.

Reliance on containment, deterrence and pressure short of force remains unsettling to Americans who seek closure in conflict and suspect that restraint betrays fecklessness. Force has the allure of apparent decisiveness. But the greatest military philosopher, Carl von Clausewitz, warned, "In war the result is never final." Unless victor and vanquished come to agreement on a peacetime order, peace will not endure. Military action might at best suppress Iran's nuclear ambitions temporarily; at worst, and no less probably, an attack could make them more intense and more dangerous.

| *"President Bush promised that America's words [declaring war on terrorism] would be credible. And he has proved true to his word."*

The War on Terror Is Strengthening America's Global Credibility

Condoleezza Rice

In the following viewpoint Condoleezza Rice contends that terrorism is threatening freedom worldwide. According to her, President George W. Bush's war on terror has set out to meet this threat and continue to spread democracy throughout the globe. So far, as Rice attests, the war has run some terrorist organizations to ground, felled two terror-supporting regimes, and planted seeds of democracy in the Middle East. Rice notes that the "world is watching" and that the victories achieved by America and its allies will pave the way to a better, safer world. Condoleezza Rice was Bush's national security adviser when she made these comments. She is currently the secretary of state.

Condoleezza Rice, "National Security Advisor Dr. Condoleezza Rice Discusses War on Terror at McConnell Center for Political Leadership," White House: Office of the Press Secretary, March 8, 2004. www.whitehouse.gov.

As you read, consider the following questions:

1. According to Rice, what are the three pillars of George W. Bush's foreign policy?

2. Who is A.Q. Khan and what is he reputed to have done, according to the author?

3. What advances toward democracy does Rice say have been made in Afghanistan and Iraq?

We live in an age of terror, in which ruthless enemies seek to destroy not only our nation and not only to destroy all free nations but to destroy freedom as a way of life. Yet we also live in an age of great opportunities to increase cooperation among the world's great powers and to spread the benefits of democracy and tolerance and freedom throughout the world. The defense of freedom has never been more necessary and the opportunity for freedom's triumph has never been greater.

In these challenging times, America is fortunate enough to have a leader like President George W. Bush and I am proud to serve him. President Bush's foreign policy is a bold new vision that draws inspiration from the ideas that have guided American foreign policy at its best: That democracies must never lack the will or the means to meet and defeat freedom's enemies, that America's power and purpose must be used to defend freedom, and that the spread of democracy leads to lasting peace.

This vision stands on three pillars. First, America will defend the peace by opposing and preventing violence by terrorists and outlaw regimes. Second, we will preserve the peace by fostering an era of good relations among the world's great powers. And third, we will extend the peace by seeking to extend the benefits of freedom and prosperity across the globe.

The very day of the September 11 [2001] attacks—as smoke still rose from the Pentagon, and the rubble of the Twin Towers, and that field in Pennsylvania—President Bush told his advisors that the United States faced a new kind of war, and that the strategy of our government would be to take the fight directly to the terrorists. That night, he announced to the world that the United States would make no distinction between the terrorists and the states that harbor them. President Bush promised that America's words would be credible. And he has proved true to his word.

Since that day, more than two-thirds of [the terrorist organization] al-Qaida's known leadership have been captured or killed. The rest are on the run—permanently. And we are working with governments around the world to bring to justice al-Qaida's associates—from Jemya Islamiya in Indonesia, to Abu Sayef in the Philippines, to Ansar al-Islam in Iraq. Under President Bush's leadership, the United States and our allies have ended terror regimes in Afghanistan and Iraq. All regimes are on notice—supporting terror is not a viable strategy for the long term.

Stopping the Proliferation of Weapons of Mass Destruction

And, of course, we must face our worst nightmare: The possibility of sudden, secret attack by chemical, biological, radiological, or nuclear weapons and the coming together of the terrorist threat with weapons of mass destruction. September 11 made clear our enemies' goals and provided painful experience of how far they are willing to go to achieve them. We cannot afford to allow the spread of weapons of mass destruction to continue. . . .

The former Iraqi regime was not only a state sponsor of terror. It was also for many years one of the world's premier WMD-producing states. For twelve years, Iraq's former dictator [Saddam Hussein] defied the international community, refusing to disarm, or to account for his illegal weapons and programs. We know he had both because he used chemical weapons against Iran and against his own people. Because, long after those attacks, he admitted having stocks and programs to UN inspectors. The world gave Saddam one last chance to disarm. He did not and now he is out of power.

The President's strong policies are leading other regimes to turn from the path of seeking weapons of mass murder. Diplomacy succeeded in Libya—in part, because no one can now doubt the resolve and purpose of the United States and our allies. The President's policy gives regimes a clear choice— they can choose to pursue dangerous weapons at great peril or they can renounce such weapons and begin the process of rejoining the international community. . . .

As we advance a broad non-proliferation agenda, we also recognize that determined proliferators cannot always be stopped by diplomacy alone. But they can be stopped. Through the President's Proliferation Security Initiative, the United States and a growing number of global partners are searching ships carrying suspect cargo, and—where necessary—are seizing dangerous materials. [In February 2004], the President also announced new proposals to close a loophole that undermines the Nuclear Nonproliferation Treaty, to strengthen antiproliferation laws and norms and tighten enforcement. We must strengthen the world's ability to keep dangerous weapons out of the hands of outlaw regimes.

We now know, however, that there are two paths to weapons of mass destruction—secretive and dangerous states that pursue them, and shadowy private networks and individuals who also traffic in these materials, motivated by greed or fanaticism or both. And often these paths meet. The world recently learned of the network headed by A.Q. Khan, the father of Pakistan's nuclear weapons program. For years, Khan and his associates sold nuclear technology and know-how to some of the world's most dangerous regimes, including North Korea and Iran. Working with intelligence officials from the United Kingdom and other nations, we unraveled the Khan network and are putting an end to its criminal enterprise. Together, the civilized nations of the world will bring to justice those who traffic in deadly weapons, shut down their labs, seize their materials, and freeze their assets. . . .

America Seeks to Advance Freedom

As we move forward with this ambitious agenda, we must never lose sight of a central truth: Lasting peace and long-term security are only possible through the advance of prosperity, liberty, and human dignity. The War on Terror—like the Cold War—is as much a conflict of visions as a struggle of armed force. The terrorists offer suicide, death, and pseudo-religious tyranny. America and our allies seek to advance the cause of liberty and defend the dignity of every person. We seek, in President Bush's words, "the advance of freedom, and the peace that freedom brings."

That means, above all, addressing what leading Arab Intellectuals have called the "freedom deficit" in the Middle East. The stakes could not be higher. If the Middle East is to leave behind stagnation, tyranny, and violence for export, then freedom must flourish in every corner of the region.

That is why the United States is pursuing a forward strategy of freedom for the Middle East. Freedom must be freely chosen, and we will seek out and work with those in the Middle East who believe in the values, habits, and institutions of liberty. We will work with those who desire to see the rule of law, freedom of the press, religious liberty, limits on the power of the state, and economic opportunity thrive in their own nations. And we will encourage the full participation of women. . . .

Success So Far

Iraq and Afghanistan are vanguards of this effort to spread democracy and tolerance and freedom throughout the Greater Middle East. Fifty million people have been liberated from two of the most brutal and dangerous tyrannies of our time.

Global Cooperation in the Fight Against Terrorism

The metaphor of war should not blind Americans to the fact that suppressing terrorism will take years of patient, unspectacular cooperation with other countries in areas such as intelligence sharing, police work, tracing financial flows, and border controls. In the wake of 9/11, the U.S. helped create the UN Counter-Terrorism Committee to co-ordinate international law enforcement efforts, and to deny financing and safe haven for Al Qaeda and other terrorist networks. Many nations have cooperated with the U.S. on these efforts, despite differences over Iraq, because it is in their national security interest to do so. As a result of this unprecedented multilateral collaboration, the financial resources available to Al Qaeda have been reduced, and the operations of the terrorist network have been disrupted. The world community has frozen over $100,000,000 in potential terrorist financial assets. More than 3,000 suspected terrorists have been taken into custody in a wide array of countries, including the United Kingdom, France, Germany, Italy, Jordan, Saudi Arabia, Spain, Pakistan, and Turkey.

David Cortright, "Creating a More Secure America,"
USA Today *magazine, July 2004.*

With the help of over sixty nations, the Iraqi and Afghan peoples are now struggling to build democracies, under difficult conditions, in the rocky soil of the Middle East.

In January [2004], Afghanistan approved a new and progressive constitution. And later [that] year, the Afghan people [held] national elections. Every day Iraqis take more responsibility for their nation's security—from guarding facilities, to policing their streets, to rebuilding the infrastructure that Saddam Hussein neglected for decades. The Iraqi people are making daily progress toward democracy. We are working with Iraqis and the United Nations to prepare for a transition to full Iraqi sovereignty. And today, members of Iraq's Governing Council signed a new Transitional Administrative Law. This historic document protects the rights of all Iraqis and moves the country toward a democratic future.

In Iraq, the work of building democracy is opposed by hold-outs among their former oppressors and by foreign terrorists. These killers seek to advance their ideology of murder by halting all progress toward democracy and a better future. They are trying to shake the will of our country and our friends. They are killing innocent Iraqis. They are sowing a reign of terror. But we and the people of Iraq will never be intimidated by thugs and assassins because America and her forces will stay the course until the job is done.

The world is watching. The failure of democracy in Iraq and Afghanistan would condemn millions to misery and embolden terrorists around the world. The defeat of terror and the success of freedom in those nations will serve the interests of our Nation, because free nations do not sponsor terror and do not breed the ideologies of murder. And success will serve our ideals, as free and democratic governments in Iraq and Afghanistan inspire hope and encourage reform throughout the greater Middle East. We cannot falter, and we will not fail.

A Better World of the Future

The work of building democracy in these nations is hard, and success will require the work of a generation. Winning the Cold War was not easy, either—and it took forty years—but the free world's alliance of strength and conviction prevailed, because we never abandoned our values or our responsibilities. As in the Cold War, progress may at times seem halting and uneven. Times of the greatest strategic importance can also be times of great turbulence. It is always easier for Presidents, no less than citizens, to do the expected thing, to follow the accepted path. Boldness is always criticized; change is always suspect. Yet Presidents from Teddy and Franklin Roosevelt, to Harry Truman, to Ronald Reagan knew that history is the final judge. And I can tell you, like those Presidents, this President knows that his obligation is not to the daily headlines, but to securing the peace and that it is history that will be the final judge. . . .

That harvest—a safer, freer, better world—is no less our hope for the decisions the United States and our allies and friends are making today. Realizing this vision may take decades. It certainly will not happen on my watch or on this President's watch. It will require a commitment of many years.

But the effort and the wait will be worth it.

> *"Years after September 11, Islamist terrorists remain a threat, . . . anti-Americanism has intensified in Europe and the Middle East, and our traditional allies are increasingly distrustful of U.S. leadership."*

The War on Terror Is Undermining America's Global Credibility

Paul Starr, Michael Tomasky, and Robert Kuttner

Paul Starr is a professor of sociology at Princeton University. Michael Tomasky is executive editor and Robert Kuttner is co-editor of the American Prospect, *a liberal newsmagazine. In the following viewpoint these authors argue that President George W. Bush's war on terror has weakened America's global alliances and proven the nation's willingness to act unilaterally. Although Starr, Tomasky, and Kuttner believe terrorists must be dealt with swiftly and occasionally with force, they claim that the Bush administration is using the war on terror to justify the overthrow of unfriendly regimes that have no clear connection to terrorism.*

Paul Starr, Michael Tomasky, and Robert Kuttner, "The Liberal Uses of Power: Clarity in Dealing with Terrorism, Yes; and Also in Living up to Our Highest Ideals," *American Prospect*, vol. 16, no. 3, March 2005, pp. 20-22. Copyright 2005 The American Prospect, Inc. All rights reserved. Reproduced with permission from *The American Prospect*, 11 Beacon Street, Suite 1120, Boston, MA 02108.

Such reckless power mongering has damaged U.S. credibility, the authors contend, and deprived foreign policy of the fruits of international cooperation.

As you read, consider the following questions:

1. In Starr, Tomasky, and Kuttner's view, if the United States is facing a "substantial, immediate, and provable threat," what does the nation have the "right and the obligation" to do?
2. In the authors' opinion, what two nonmilitary measures should the U.S. government pursue to counter anti-American Islamic fundamentalism?
3. According to Starr, Tomasky, and Kuttner, what two consequences will the United States suffer if it follows its unilateral, militarized foreign policy agenda?

It is a shame there will never be a debate about foreign policy between the George W. Bush who ran for president in 2000 and the one who now occupies the office. As a candidate [in 2000], Bush said that the United States should act as a "humble nation" toward the rest of the world and avoid any involvement of our armed forces in nation building. He could have had a lively argument with the current president over the use of the military for nation building in Iraq, and he might have raised an eyebrow over the president's declaration, at his second inauguration, that it is American policy to "seek and support the growth of democratic movements and institutions in every nation and culture, with the ultimate goal of ending tyranny in our world." The original Bush appealed to an insular Americanism with a constricted conception of the national interest; the new Bush appeals to a missionary vision of America's role. As much as the first understated America's obligations, the second risks overextending them. In our hypothetical debate, the two would nonetheless find they had a lot in common: an us-and-them view of good and evil in the world; an indifference toward allies and international institutions; and, of course, a readiness to use force.

America's Foreign-Policy Foibles

Bush's worldview and instincts served the country well enough in the immediate aftermath of [the] September 11, [2001, terrorist attacks upon America] at least with respect to foreign policy: The terrorists were indeed evil, and the war in Afghanistan was a fully justified response. But the limitations of the president's approach to the world have been evident ever since. He undertook the Iraq War on false and misleading premises, with overoptimistic expectations and inadequate post-invasion plans, undermining our credibility, alliances, and focus on al-Qaeda. It was only as his original rationale for invading Iraq weakened and ultimately collapsed that he reframed the war as a crusade for democracy. If the Iraqis now establish a stable, democratic government, it will be a great positive step for their country and the region, but there is a considerable risk of an unintended and perverse result: a pro-Iranian Islamic state hostile to liberal values and American interests and willing to hold free elections only as long as they produce results acceptable to the Shia clerical hierarchy.

Moreover, even if Iraq's government does not go the way of Iran, the Iraq War will not have removed the perils that led to the direct engagement of the United States in the Islamic world. Three and a half years after September 11, Islamist terrorists remain a threat, U.S. military forces are stretched to the limit, anti-Americanism has intensified in Europe and the Middle East, and our traditional allies are increasingly distrustful of U.S. leadership and are setting an independent path in foreign affairs.

In other ways, the Bush administration has also undermined American power and influence. Its fiscal policies have created a dangerous dependence on foreign borrowing to fi-

The International Community Is Distancing Itself from America

The causes of our loss of respect and influence go much deeper than our unilateral tendencies. . . . On a global plane the United States may still be the world's only superpower. Viewed, however, at the level of our key relationships with Europe, Russia, China and Japan, in each case we need these countries as much as or more than they need us— whether it be for money and troops for Iraq and Afghanistan, diplomatic support on Iran and North Korea, or capital to pay for our military budget and our consumption and investment needs. . . . Just a decade ago, the great majority of Europeans wanted to keep the United States involved in Europe; now they want to keep us at a distance in order to insulate themselves from the instability and hatred that Washington's policies are creating in the nearby Arab world. American relations with Asia have similarly been transformed, with much of Asia trying to avoid getting drawn into Washington's "war on terrorism" and trying to prevent the United States from acting precipitately against North Korea.

Sherle R. Schwenninger, "A World Neglected:
The Foreign Policy Debate We Should Be Having,"
Nation, *October 18, 2004.*

nance our budget and trade deficits, and its energy policies have increased our dependence on foreign oil. The inevitable result is a double standard vis-a-vis China and unsavory Middle Eastern regimes. Bush's defenders like to portray liberals, particularly those who opposed the Iraq War, as weak and unserious about national security. But the truth is that the war itself and other administration policies are weakening our power and security, undermining our alliances and freedom of action. . . .

Islamist Terrorism Is a Real Threat

The first imperative of America's defense and foreign policy, however, is to protect our security, and today Islamist terrorists with global reach pose the greatest immediate threat to our lives and liberties. We—the United States, the advanced world generally, and liberals in particular, who value the rule of law, equality, open-mindedness, tolerance, and secularism—face a struggle with the jihadists [Muslim religious warriors] that we have no alternative but to win. The fanatical nature of Islamic fundamentalism and the terrorism it has spawned should be clear to all of us. Its goals for the world are so profoundly inimical to ours, and its methods so intolerable, that negotiation, of the sort the United States engaged in with its best-known ideological foe of the last century [the Soviet Union], is impossible. The terrorists not only threaten liberal values in Islamic countries; they also imperil the survival of freedom in ours. If they launch further major attacks on our shores, the [civil liberties–restricting] PATRIOT Act and [the imprisonment of suspected terrorists at] Guantanamo Bay [in Cuba] will likely prove mere prelude to much worse. Defending our liberties and best traditions at home, then, depends directly on defeating terrorism abroad.

Our call for clarity in dealing with terrorism reflects the urgency of a historical moment that demands we sort out the things that are genuinely important—the conditions that are necessary for the flourishing of liberal values. The lines that separate liberal principle from fundamentalist design have rarely been clearer, and they are lines that liberals must defend unambiguously, and with force when necessary. President Bush has been wrong, often calamitously so, about many things, but he is right that America must do all it can to prevent another 9-11. When facing a substantial, immediate, and provable threat, the United States has both the right and the obligation to strike preemptively and, if need be, unilaterally against terrorists or states that support them.

© Copyright 2004 Patrick Chappatte. All rights reserved.

Because of the direct threat of Islamic terrorism to liberal values, liberals ought to be particularly conscious of the need for an effective defense. But some have drawn the wrong lessons from history. Beginning with the Vietnam War, many progressives instinctively opposed any assertion of American power. They pointed, accurately enough, to instances where the United States engineered the overthrow of democratically elected left-wing governments while supporting dictators of convenience, such as the shah of Iran. After [Iraqi dictator] Saddam Hussein invaded Kuwait in 1990, too few liberals saw that a war was a just and necessary response. Many, however, were more favorable to the use of force later in the decade, when [President] Bill Clinton's interventions in Bosnia and Kosovo stopped ethnic cleansing and prevented Serbian aggression from spiraling into a wider war in the region. September 11 solidified the growing conviction among liberals that the United States had to be prepared to use force to defend security and liberal values.

Still, some on the left opposed the war in Afghanistan, and just as Vietnam led to an overly broad rejection of force, so the misconceived invasion of Iraq now lends credence to a reflexive hostility to American power. We understand the historical roots of this mistrust, but today's world presents problems that require different habits of mind. The real problem in Afghanistan was not that the United States sent in troops but that it did not send in enough to complete the job and capture or kill Osama bin Laden. Iraq was the wrong war waged the wrong way; it began on false premises and may end badly—but we can neither walk away from it nor become complacent about other dangers. . . .

Listening to the World

Where terrorism is concerned, preemptive, unilateral, and decisive force may be legitimate. The right of preemption, however, is not the same as a blanket entitlement to preventive war to overthrow hostile regimes that pose no immediate threat, particularly where other countermeasures, international in scope, may be sufficient to achieve the purpose. As the Iraq experience shows, mistakes in preventive war have enormous costs in the lost credibility of American leadership, lost resources, and, not least of all, lost lives. The United States has unmatched military power, but our armed forces are relatively limited in numbers, and even this country will find itself overextended if it tries to use force to squelch all potential threats.

The larger problem, moreover, arises from the environment that has fostered terrorism. The jihadists can lay claim, it is sad to observe, to deep intellectual roots in the Muslim world, the indirect support of schools and cultural institutions, and a significant body of public opinion. A resolution of the Israeli-Palestinian conflict would help remove a major source of inflammation between Islamic fundamentalism and the West, but the terrorist threat wouldn't end there. We have a stake in the success of liberalizing educational and cultural forces in the Islamic world, and we ought to be using our resources and influence to bolster those movements. . . .

As the sole superpower in the world, the United States is in an extraordinary position to shape the rules and practices of the international system. That system can augment our power, as it did during the Cold War, through a system of partnerships with other countries, based on consultation and joint decision making. Instead, under Bush's leadership, the United States is intent on setting a unilateral course, which other countries are welcome to join if they accept our terms. That approach appeals to a deep, conservative nationalist tendency in America. From the insular conservatism that Bush advocated in 2000, it is but a short step to the missionary neoconservatism that he espouses today. Both are dismissive of a cooperative international framework. But acting unilaterally, the United States will face twin problems of its own making at home and abroad. First, as in Iraq, American taxpayers will assume an outsized share of the military burden of maintaining world order. And second, we will continue generating hostility elsewhere in the world and spurring other countries, including our traditional allies, to do what they have already begun: strengthen their own partnerships, like the European Union, separate from and perhaps increasingly in opposition to us. The liberal alternative to Bush is not to lessen our power but to listen to the world and, in the process, to add to the power that we and other liberal democracies can marshal to strengthen our security and freedom and to get on with the forgotten agenda of protecting the global environment and alleviating the poverty and misery that are still the fate of hundreds of millions of the world's people.

Periodical Bibliography

The following articles have been selected to supplement the diverse views presented in this chapter.

David Cortright — "Creating a More Secure America: By Employing Cooperative Engagement—the Perfect Antidote to the Bush Administration's Insistence on Preemptive Unilateralism—the U.S. Can Bring Its Security Doctrine More in Line with Global Realities," *USA Today* magazine, July 2004.

Ivan Eland — "It's What We Do: The Administration Says the Terrorists Hate Us for Who We Are. But That Isn't What the Terrorists Say—or What the Record Shows," *American Prospect*, January 2006.

William Norman Grigg — "Is Iran Next? The Bush Administration's Crusade to 'Democratize' the Middle East Is Zeroing in on Iran's Nuclear Ambitions. The Result Could Be Devastating—but the Worst Need Not Happen," *New American*, March 6, 2006.

Frederick W. Kagan — "Fighting to Win: With the Proper Strategy, Victory in Iraq Is Far More Likely than People Think," *Weekly Standard*, December 19, 2005.

Stanley Reed — "Hearts, Minds, and Mistakes: How Can the U.S. Win Back the Goodwill It Lost in Iraq? First, Empower the Iraqis," *Business Week*, April 26, 2004.

David B.J. Rivkin and Lee A. Casey — "Why We're There: We Went into Iraq, and Persist There Now, for Sound Reasons," *National Review*, December 31, 2005.

Fernando R. Teson — "Ending Tyranny in Iraq," *Ethics & International Affairs*, October 2005.

Howard Zinn — "Our War on Terrorism," *Progressive*, November 2004.

CHAPTER 3

How Are American Economic Policies Affecting Trade and Foreign Aid?

Chapter Preface

Throughout the twentieth century, technological advancements have speeded globalization. Globalization encompasses a variety of changes, all sharing the common factor of increased connectivity between people of different and distant nations. In general, individuals are able to move more freely across national boundaries and communicate over great distances with more ease and frequency; however, one of the most significant and controversial components of globalization is trade.

The international economy has grown ever more interdependent as foreign markets open up and shipping services deliver goods in increasingly shorter time. The United States and its trade policies have led this economic globalization. U.S. trade policies are contingent upon an open market system and free trade in which private corporations orchestrate the flow of capital, and barriers, such as tariffs, to restrict trade are limited. Often, trade agreements with the United States promise more than simply the prospect of economic trade with America. Proponents of free trade often cite the rise of democratic political institutions in countries with open markets and better political relations with the United States. Taib Fassi Fihri, associate minister of foreign affairs and cooperation for the Kingdom of Morocco, said of his country's trade relations with the United States, "I regard a free trade agreement as a significant encouragement to the economic and political reforms initiated by the Kingdom, and a powerful tool in the development of bilateral relations."

Opponents of globalized trade policies dominated by U.S. interests argue that these systems create more problems than they solve. Some view free trade as a means for American companies to dump excess goods into fledgling foreign economies and thus swamp the growth of competition. Others note that Western corporations often move production into less-developed nations to exploit cheap labor and lax environmental laws. Instead of boosting impoverished populations, these two forces may drive down wages and enslave workers to foreign conglomerates. For example, studies have shown that after the implementation of the North American Free Trade Agreement, the poverty rate in Mexico has risen instead of diminished.

While the impact of free trade policies is an unsettled issue, the progress of economic globalization is undeniable. In the following chapter the authors examine specific U.S. trade policies and foreign aid strategies and debate the influence of the United States on the global economy.

| "Money is best spent on those countries that rule justly, invest in their people, and encourage economic freedom."

The Millennium Challenge Account Is an Effective Foreign Aid Policy

Paul V. Applegarth

The Millennium Challenge Corporation (MCC) was created in January 2004 to administer the Millennium Challenge Account (MCA), a new American aid program with the goal of reducing world poverty by funding foreign governments that commit to sound economic policies, ruling justly, and investing in their people. The following viewpoint is excerpted from Paul V. Applegarth's testimony to the Senate Foreign Relations Committee, in which he presents the goals of the MCC and provides evidence of positive progress that has been made since the program's inception. Applegarth argues that the MCC provides an excellent opportunity to reduce world poverty because it encourages reforms that will ensure proper implementation of economic aid. Applegarth is currently the CEO of Value Enhancement International, an international consulting and investment firm that works in emerging markets.

Paul V. Applegarth, "MCC CEO Paul Applegarth's Testimony before the House International Relations Committee," Millenium Challenge Corporation, April 26, 2005. www .mca.gov. Reproduced by permission of the author.

As you read, consider the following questions:

1. What are the policies that "support poverty reduction and economic growth," according to Paul Applegarth?

2. What types of reform does Applegarth state that the Millennium Challenge Corporation has prompted in countries hoping to receive assistance funds?

3. As Applegarth states, how long did it take Madagascar to create a workable compact with the MCC?

On January 23, 2004, the MCC was established to administer the MCA, an innovative new foreign assistance program designed to more effectively focus U.S. development assistance on poverty reduction.

MCC is built on the common sense idea that foreign aid yields better results when invested where countries have put in place policies that support poverty reduction and economic growth—policies such as good governance, investment in health and education and an enabling environment for entrepreneurs. Indeed, MCC is about helping these countries help themselves.

In addition, MCC and international development assistance are not only about bringing the best of America to our relationship with the world, but as a key component of U.S. national security, as the 9/11 Commission Report recommends: "A comprehensive U.S. strategy to counter terrorism should include economic policies that encourage development, more open societies, and opportunities for people to improve the lives of their families and to enhance prospects for their children's future." . . .

Early Successes Reveal the MCC's Potential

In May 2004, MCC had been in existence for less than four months, yet had significant milestones to report. Candidate countries had been identified, and the Board had already selected the first 16 eligible countries to submit proposals for funding.

By mid 2004, less than eight weeks after MCC's Board had selected them, MCC teams had visited all 16 of our eligible countries. We are continuing to spend time on the ground in virtually every country and I can assure you that considerable progress is being made.

We count among our recent accomplishments [in 2005] the MCC Board of Directors approval of our first Compact with the country of Madagascar for just under $110 million.... The Madagascar Compact marks an important step forward for the MCC. But it is only a beginning. There are many more countries working hard for the opportunity to sign a Compact. There are hundreds of millions of lives that we are in a position to improve, provided we have adequate means.

We have already notified Congress of our intention to negotiate Compacts with Honduras, Georgia, Nicaragua, and Cape Verde, and—subject to successful negotiations, favorable due diligence results and Board approval—we hope to be in a position to sign Compacts with each of them by this summer [2005; indeed, by the end of August 2005, the MCC had committed approximately one billion dollars to five different Compacts]. In short, while it is difficult to be precise about our schedule, we anticipate that Compact approvals will proceed at a rapid pace....

A New Approach to Reducing Poverty

The concepts behind the MCC are bold and, as a package, unique. More importantly, they make sense for U.S. development assistance and for the countries we are helping. In 2004, the United States government created MCC as an alternative to what has previously been done in the field of foreign assistance....

Through the years, the United States and others have devoted considerable funding to alleviating the effects of global poverty. Regrettably, however, there is far too little to be seen in terms of poverty reduction in relation to dollars spent. The MCC offers a new development assistance approach that requires measurable results for aid investment. We have learned that simply giving large sums of money away without quantifiable targets is not the most productive means of providing foreign assistance.

We know now that money is best spent on those countries that rule justly, invest in their people, and encourage economic freedom. This is the environment that can use the goodwill of the United States and translate it into sustainable economic growth. The MCC was established to make this happen in the poorest countries in the world.

The MCC Encourages Reform

Investing is always a risk when a measurable and positive outcome is desired. Bill Gates [CEO of Microsoft] said that "giving money away is a far greater challenge than earning it." The MCC has eagerly accepted this challenge. We have taken on the responsibility of helping fortify the desired results and of assisting in the measurement of them—we expect the United States will be proud of the results we achieve.

In fact, the success of the MCC has already begun, as our role in the foreign assistance arena has yielded results even before spending money. Early indications tell us that our process is working. Morocco and Vanuatu have consulted NGOs [nongovernmental organizations] and the business sector for the first time. The MCA incentive has also prompted reform; anecdotal evidence points to a strong MCA role. One country, for example, passed four pieces of anticorruption legislation and began enforcement, in the hope of receiving MCC assistance. [Two years after] the announcement of MCA indicators in February 2003, the median number of "days to start a business" has dropped from 61 to 46 in MCA candidate countries. Many countries have targeted corruption—a primary MCC indicator—and are making strides to reduce corruption within

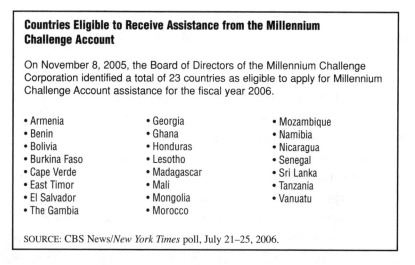

Countries Eligible to Receive Assistance from the Millennium Challenge Account

On November 8, 2005, the Board of Directors of the Millennium Challenge Corporation identified a total of 23 countries as eligible to apply for Millennium Challenge Account assistance for the fiscal year 2006.

• Armenia	• Georgia	• Mozambique
• Benin	• Ghana	• Namibia
• Bolivia	• Honduras	• Nicaragua
• Burkina Faso	• Lesotho	• Senegal
• Cape Verde	• Madagascar	• Sri Lanka
• East Timor	• Mali	• Tanzania
• El Salvador	• Mongolia	• Vanuatu
• The Gambia	• Morocco	

SOURCE: CBS News/*New York Times* poll, July 21–25, 2006.

their governments. Bangladesh's finance minister, Saifur Rahman, while proposing a tough program targeting corruption, cited his country's exclusion from MCA eligibility specifically as an example of the heavy price his country was paying for being branded a corrupt country. One official from an eligible country said, "even if we receive less than requested, the intangibles gained from taking control of our own development destiny are the most important part of the process."

The MCC Promotes Democratic Ideals

MCC believes in country ownership. We believe that countries, no matter how poor, should have the opportunity to create a real program of economic growth for the benefit of their country—reflecting their priorities which address the needs of the people of their country—not just their government's or ours. Countries maintain their autonomy while working with the MCC and, through mutual effort, a Compact takes shape.

Yet the MCC does more than provide assistance; it disseminates and encourages democratic ideals. The monetary incentive of the MCA is incredibly powerful. When a respectable but weak country is provided the means to grow and develop, the national security interests of the United States are better protected.

The MCC has great responsibility. We have a responsibility to reduce poverty in some of the poorest countries of the world and we have a responsibility to the American people to invest their money wisely with achievable positive results. . . . MCC also has the authority under provision 609(g) of its legislation to make disbursements to eligible countries to facilitate development and implementation of the Compact.

Our Compacts are implemented over three to five years, but, as directed by Congress, we obligate all our money up front and disburse as needed based on quantifiable benchmarks. This is part of the strength of the MCA and what will make us especially effective. Up-front monetary commitment helps motivate and support policy reform, assures all countries involved that substantial development progress can be made, that programs can be administered effectively, and that poverty will be reduced. . . .

New Programs Take Time to Implement

I also want to take this opportunity formally to address and respond to comments I have heard regarding the MCC timeline—specifically the notion that MCC has been off to a slow start.

The Millennium Challenge compact development process is thorough and it has never been done. As a point of reference, in the private sector, when an investment proposal is received, the parties have been through the process before, the objectives are known (e.g., financial return or creditworthiness) and the management organization and implementation plan are known.

In contrast, the MCC and our countries are going through this process for the first time. Together we must identify our objectives, how we will measure results, and work to develop detailed implementation plans. We do not want the efficacy of the mission to be reduced because we are rushing to meet artificial deadlines or rushing money out the door. We want to do things right and we want to do them right the first time. But we also want to do the right thing fast.

My experience has taught me that you are doing well in the private sector if it takes only four to five months from the time a sound and well supported proposal is received until an investment is made—and I am sure many of you can attest to this. I am told the World Bank takes an average of 18 months to make a lending decision. We received the first draft of Madagascar's Compact proposal in October 2004. In only six months, Madagascar and the MCC have succeeded in creating a workable Compact that will reduce poverty through economic growth. Certainly, this is a good accomplishment by any standard. . . .

The Millennium Challenge Corporation is not a quick-fix to poverty. We put substantial time into Compact development and review to ensure that the U.S. investment will make a definitive and positive impact on the poorest countries in the world. We are fiduciaries [trustees in charge] of the money Congress has appropriated. We remain committed to making sure the American taxpayers' investment is used wisely.

> *"The approach to the selectivity on which the MCA so heavily relies is very troubling."*

The Millennium Challenge Account Is a Flawed Foreign Aid Policy

Aldo Caliari

Aldo Caliari is a project coordinator at the Center of Concern, a Catholic social justice organization. In the following viewpoint Caliari questions the efficacy of the Millennium Challenge Account (MCA), a method of distributing foreign aid based on receiver nations' commitment to good governance and sound economic policies. Caliari argues that the method of selecting such countries is problematic because the criteria are subjective and unreliable.

As you read, consider the following questions:

1. What are the two exceptions Caliari cites that would keep a country from receiving aid under the Millennium Challenge Account guidelines?

2. What are some of the problematic contradictions in the selection process that the author points out?

Aldo Caliari, "The Millennium Challenge Account: Unlearning How to Make Aid Work?" *Center Focus*, no. 160, June 2003. www.coc.org. Reproduced by permission.

3. According to Caliari, what is the potential "core problem" in using an indicator of good governance when assessing which countries receive economic aid?

In March 2002, a few days before the Financing for Development Summit (FFD), President [George W.] Bush announced his initiative to create the Millennium Challenge Account (MCA). The proposal called for gradually increasing U.S. overseas development assistance over a period of three years, beginning in FY [fiscal year] 2004. By FY 2006, the annual amount of U.S. foreign aid would have increased about 50% to around US$5 billion. One distinctive feature of the proposal was that the recipient countries would only be selected from among those countries deemed to have a policy environment adequate to ensure that aid would be effective. Although the criteria to select the recipients of the MCA funds were not given at the time, the Bush Administration announced that the recipients would be those countries that were committed to 1) sound economic policies (economic freedom), 2) ruling justly (good governance), and 3) investing in their people (health and education).

The announcement of the MCA was aimed at appeasing criticism of the obstructionist position that the U.S. had taken throughout the rest of the FFD conference process by showing some willingness to make a concession, even if only in unilateral terms. In fact, the announcement received a lot of attention from the media from all over the world [who were] gathered in Monterrey, Mexico for the FFD Summit. However, the very broad language used in the initial official speeches made it difficult, if not impossible, for anyone to make an objective assessment of the potential impacts of the MCA on poverty reduction and on development in developing countries. . . . Since the MCA was unveiled, civil society organizations have been engaging significantly in the discussion around the selection process and criteria for MCA recipients. Today, much more is known about these criteria because the Bush Administration has sent to Congress a concrete legislative proposal. The proposal, presenting the most detailed description of the MCA selection criteria available so far, offers reasons to be deeply concerned about its likely impact on the recipient countries.

The Selection Process of the MCA Is Problematic

According to the proposal, the MCA recipients will be selected based on a measurement of performance according to 16 criteria grouped into three clusters, each of them covering one of the policy areas originally outlined by the president's March 2002 announcement. To qualify, a country must score above the median on half of the criteria in each policy area. There are two exceptions: for a country to qualify, its inflation must be below a pre-specified rate and a country not scoring above the median in the anti-corruption criterion cannot qualify.

The approach to the selectivity on which the MCA so heavily relies is very troubling. Such selectivity implies that aid is more effective in producing results when directed to countries that have in place "good policies" which is, of course, true. The question, however, gets tricky as soon as one begins trying to determine what those "good" policies are and who has the right and the knowledge to decide what is "good." For example, there is widespread agreement today that there is no such thing as a universal model of development. Different countries have developed using different policies. Hence, there is need to allow countries the policy space to discern their own mix of policies, tailored to their respective endowments and their social and political circumstances. But the MCA assumes that there is a one-size-fits-all set of policies that is "good" for all countries everywhere and acts as a precondition for growth.

It is also widely accepted that policies can only be successful when they are owned by the government and the society in a country. However, it is clear that under the MCA proposal, a country whose government and society have achieved a democratic consensus on a set of policies that they find suitable might not be eligible for aid unless the policies they "own" reflect the U.S. government's model policies.

An additional problem is that the proposed MCA selectivity does not address the contradictions among the different indicators. For example, many of the economic policies a country needs to implement to qualify under "economic freedom" can only be implemented in a climate of repression and by curtailment of the civil liberties and political freedoms that are essential to approval under the criteria for "good governance," as the experience of several developing countries has shown. As another example, "primary education completion rates," assessed under "investing in people," have declined in many countries due to implementation of budget cuts needed to meet the kind of budget deficit targets that are assessed under "economic freedom." A critical assessment of more specific MCA indicators that would be used to rate countries on each policy area is important from a social justice perspective.

The MCA Uses Misguided Economic Indicators

Some of the indicators under this cluster closely resemble the neoliberal policies that have spread through the developing world via the lending programs of the World Bank and the IMF [International Monetary Fund] for the last twenty years. Not only have such policies promoted little in terms of economic growth, but they have also led to disastrous social and environmental impacts. Some specific indicators under this cluster are:

Trade policy The proposed indicator is an index of economic freedom developed by the Heritage Foundation [a conservative public policy institute]. Using this indicator amounts to adhering to the view that trade liberalization is always conducive to growth. Yet, this notion has become severely contested even by mainstream economists who have brought to light the serious flaws of the research that underpinned it. New analyses have highlighted that, in order to have a positive impact on the economy, open trade reforms must be well-sequenced and paced, done on a selective basis, and in the context of a national development strategy.

The need to consider other factors like the availability of markets for exports, the ability of domestic industry to withstand competition, and the ability of the state to support domestic entrepreneurs and regulate unfair competition has also been highlighted.

Inflation rate Only countries with an inflation rate below 20% would be eligible for assistance. Although a low inflation is in general terms healthy for an economy, there is no consensus on how much is too much, particularly given the tradeoffs between level of inflation on the one hand and employment and growth of output on the other.

Country credit rating Country credit ratings are assessments of the policy environment in a country that are prepared by private agencies to advise investors. A crucial issue with credit-rating agencies is that, in spite of the large influence they have on investors' decisions, they remain largely unaccountable. Moreover, the lack of transparency of their assessments has become a major problem for developing countries with large stocks of foreign investment. These countries have seen their attempts to put in place policies enjoying wide support among the population thwarted by negative assessments of risk that threaten to trigger an investors' exit from the country. Using credit ratings as one of the indicators for awarding aid would institutionalize and extend the scope of the damage caused by the practices of these agencies.

The MCA Encourages Socialism

MCA encourages socialism and statism. Because it is entirely geared toward foreign governments, it will force economically devastating public-private partnerships in developing nations: if the private sector is to see any of the money it will have to be in partnership with government. There should be no doubt that these foreign governments will place additional requirements on the private firms in order to qualify for funding. Who knows how much of this money will be wasted on those companies with the best political connections to the foreign governments in power. The MCA invites political corruption by creating a slush fund at the control of foreign governments.

Ron Paul, "Reject the Millennium Challenge Account,"
May 19, 2004. www.house.gov/paul.

The MCA Subjectively Rewards Governments

The indicators under this cluster are also highly controversial. Some studies have challenged the apparently straightforward relevance of high-quality institutions to economic growth on the basis of historical analysis. Indeed, these studies show that today's developed countries became developed when they had weaker institutions than most developing countries have today. They also show that the institutions of today's developed countries have evolved in different ways and taken different shapes. So, even if we agreed that good governance is a necessary precondition for economic development, that does not necessarily imply an Anglo-American model of governance.

Leaving aside this debate, a core problem with the measurement of good governance is the potential it offers for subjective and politicized judgments. When the country issuing the judgments has, like the U.S., a history of using aid to reward allies and promote national geopolitical goals, an added dose of skepticism is in order. Measurement of governance, thus, poses significant challenges. How to discriminate between the institutions that may be legitimate in a particular country's social, cultural and political environment and those that belong to a particular, Anglo-American model of governance? How to ensure that the assessment is objective across countries? How to differentiate between governance problems that are due to lack of a government's commitment to certain policies and those that are inherent to the poverty level of a country? The fact that with two indicators, "civil liberties" and "political freedoms," the proposed indexes are developed by the U.S. conservative organization Freedom House and are based on a paradigm that excludes economic, social, cultural, and communal rights raises serious concerns in this regard.

Of particular importance under this cluster is the criterion on corruption because ... it is a pass/fail indicator. Corruption would be measured according to an index developed by the World Bank Institute. This index has been criticized for the unreliability of the data on which it is based, and the World Bank team that prepared it called repeatedly for caution in its application. There has also been note of the fact that it only emphasizes corruption in the public sector, while leaving unmentioned the dubious conduct of the private companies that are on the other end of the bribes reportedly received by public officials.

Absolute Outcomes Are Unreliable Indicators of Success

The indicators in this area are also not without controversy. Two of them, the primary education completion rate and the immunization rates for some specified illnesses, focus on absolute outcomes. This means that the indicators do not differentiate between internal and external factors responsible for failure. Governments implementing externally-imposed structural adjustment policies requiring the privatization of health and education, which had such negative impacts on the access to these services among the people in poverty, might paradoxically end up punished for the failure of these imposed policies to achieve adequate educational and health levels.

The MCA Ignores Historical Lessons

The Millennium Challenge Account proposal comes at a time of widespread declines in overseas development assistance. Without a doubt, as its implementation advances, it is not only going to raise U.S. aid levels, it is also going to have a strong impact on the way that U.S. development assistance is delivered. And because of the U.S. position in the world, the MCA is also likely to catalyze changes in the way that multilateral development assistance, in general, is delivered. It, thus, comes as a great tragedy that in such an influential initiative the Bush Administration has chosen to ignore the lessons from the past regarding what works and what does not in terms of promoting sustainable and equitable development. The real challenge is to educate citizens and civil society about the serious flaws in the Millennium Challenge Account, to promote discussion and debate in the media on these flaws and to advocate for changes in the paradigm for aid delivery.

"China's newly enriched consumers are eager to own quintessentially American products."

American Consumer Goods Sell Well in China

Jehangir S. Pocha

Jehangir S. Pocha, an American news correspondent in China, states in the following viewpoint that American brands sell well in China. Pocha explains that Chinese consumers have no experience with American brand histories, so U.S. companies are easily able to create new markets for their products in China. In addition, many American goods have increased marketability in China because they are perceived as exotic and luxurious in comparison to domestic products.

As you read, consider the following questions:

1. According to Pocha, why are Buicks a status symbol in China?

2. Why does the Chinese news do little product reporting or analysis, in the author's view?

3. According to Eddie Lu, as cited by Pocha, why does the strategy of marketing U.S. goods as prestigious luxuries work in China?

Older brands are enjoying a revival in China. The country's burgeoning but relatively unsophisticated consumer market has become an ideal resurrecting ground for older U.S. brands such as Buick cars and Lee jeans.

Capitalizing on a Desire for American Products

After years of coveting these and other American products they saw in pirated Hollywood movies or heard of from immigrant friends, China's newly enriched consumers are eager to own quintessentially American products. And American companies are proving adept at maintaining, and even increasing, their appeal in China. That's giving many older brands an unexpected life extension in what could soon be the world's largest consumer market.

"Here companies can start with a clean slate and create totally new images for a totally different audience. Many brands we are familiar with in the United States have a totally different positioning or image here," said Edward Bell, head of planning with Ogilvy & Mather Beijing, an advertising firm.

Old Brands Create a New Image

Consider Buick. In the United States, cars carrying the brand's triple shield logo are not really considered to be on the same level as BMWs and Audis. But in China, "Buick is an expensive car and has a very big name," said Yan Lili, 30, a corporate manager in Beijing. "I'd love to own one."

The difference in perception is partly due to the way the car has been marketed in China. Buicks were among the first foreign cars on Chinese roads and both the cars and their promotional campaigns impressed drivers.

American Businesses Thrive in China

China's major cities have sprouted American stores and restaurants at prodigious rates, including Starbucks, PriceSmart, Pizza Hut, McDonald's and Esprit clothing outlets. New housing compounds bear names like Orange County and Manhattan Gardens. A high-end Buick is a sought-after luxury car, a replacement for last year's Audi.

Europeans may be wont to view every Big Mac as a terrifying sign of American cultural imperialism, but Chinese have mostly welcomed the invasion—indeed they have internalized it.

In one recent survey, nearly half of all Chinese children under 12 identified McDonald's as a domestic brand.

Elisabeth Rosenthal, "Beijing Journal:
Buicks, Starbucks and Fried Chicken. Still China?"
New York Times, *February 25, 2002.*

"A midlevel U.S. product automatically falls into the higher end of the market here," Bell said. "Compared to local cars, (Buicks) are expensive. They're big and they're foreign and so they're as much of a status badge as an Audi." That's allowed Buick's manufacturer, General Motors, to recently charge Chinese customers as much as $37,000 for a Buick Regal that sold for about $23,000 in the United States.

Yet GM's Chinese buyers get a one-year warranty rather than the three-year bumper-to-bumper warranty provided to buyers in the United States. The result: GM makes about $2,000 on every Buick Regal sold in China, about 15 times its U.S. profit on each car, according to industry reports.

Chinese Middle Class
Lacks Consumer Savvy

A recent survey of 1,800 U.S. businesses in China by the American Chamber of Commerce in Beijing found that the profit margins for 42 percent of them are higher than their average worldwide margins.

One reason U.S. companies enjoy pricing freedom in China is that the country's newly created middle class has had little consumer education. There are no Ralph Naders in China, and many industries, including the auto industry, are controlled by large state-owned companies that have entered into joint ventures with foreign firms.

With the state having a vested interest in corporate profitability, the press, which is mostly controlled by the state, does little consumer reporting. Most Chinese consumers can't read the U.S. press because of China's controls on access to foreign media and the language barrier, so they have no independent perception of brands, making it easy for companies to create perceptions through marketing campaigns, Bell said.

Catering to the Chinese Market

Buick's success is partly due to GM's unique marketing campaign. GM representatives declined to be interviewed for this story, but the company's Web site says the Buick Regal was created as a "sign of respect for successful leaders. Regal is the best choice amongst the cars of the same class because Regal expresses their ways of life, their success and highly respectable positions."

Bell said that in China, the field is evenly divided between foreign companies that are trying to win over consumers in China's low-end market and those angling for its small but wealthy top-tier segments.

Some brands, such as Johnson & Johnson baby shampoo, have created different versions of their products that they sell in China for less than half the U.S. price. Others, such as [soup maker] Maggi, have used the core values of their brand to extend beyond traditional products, such as ready-to-eat soups, into new ones that serve local needs, such as ready-to-eat dumplings.

The Prestige of Foreign Goods

But several companies are also relying on Chinese consumers' penchant for conspicuous consumption to position popular U.S. brands as exclusive items.

Americans visiting Beijing are often surprised to see Haagen-Dazs ice cream for sale in the lobby of a five-star hotel, where a pint goes for $10, nearly twice as much as in the United States. "Part of the reason for such pricing is simply extra costs, such as transportation and duties," said Eddie Lu, marketing manager with Haagen-Dazs in Shanghai. But more significantly, he said, Haagen-Dazs has sidestepped its U.S. image as a premium supermarket brand to position itself as a uniquely luxurious culinary experience.

The strategy is working well because "there's a reward-yourself lifestyle here," said Lu. "People don't mind paying for prestige items, especially if they are foreign." The strategy has worked so well that Haagen-Dazs has opened several elegantly appointed ice cream cafes, where teenagers pay as much as $40 for a sundae.

Several other companies are propelling themselves up the image chain through simple changes in location and distribution strategies.

Lee jeans, which were all the rage with U.S. shoppers in the 1970s but which now sell at discount stores for about $25 apiece, have just been introduced in China as the ultimately cool American wear.

Ports1961, a leading North American fashion retailer in the 1960s, has little name recognition among young fashion-conscious shoppers today. But it's a different story in Beijing, where the company, now owned by Hong Kong's CFS International, has a store alongside those bearing more illustrious names, such as Chanel and Esprit.

"American products are struggling these days in the Chinese market."

American Consumer Goods Do Not Sell Well in China

Keith Bradsher

In the following viewpoint Keith Bradsher, Hong Kong bureau chief for the New York Times, *states that American goods do not sell well in China. Bradsher says that economists blame the problem on the declining quality of American goods and a lack of interest on the part of American companies to promote and sell goods in China.*

As you read, consider the following questions:

1. What are some of the American products Bradsher says sell "like hotcakes" in China and why?
2. According to the author, how do companies from other countries in Asia contribute to America's bilateral trade deficit with China?
3. How will the American trade deficit narrow, according to Alan Greenspan, as cited by Bradsher?

Keith Bradsher, "Made in U.S., Shunned in China," *New York Times*, November 18, 2005. p. C1. Copyright © 2005 by The New York Times Company. Reproduced by permission.

Abby Chan, a 23-year-old advertising copywriter, took a break from shopping for Levi's jeans at a mall here [in Guangzhou, China,] on [a] Wednesday evening and relaxed at a table in a Starbucks restaurant.

Aside from coffee and denim, there were not many American brand products that interested her. She covets Chanel clothing and Louis Vuitton bags, dreams of owning a BMW or Mercedes-Benz someday, and struggles to think of an American brand that appeals to her. "There are more choices for European brands, more styles, so they are more interesting," she said. . . .

But for a long list of reasons, American products are struggling these days in the Chinese market, where they have trouble measuring up to European brands and even some Chinese brands.

Declining Quality Contributes to the Bilateral Deficit

The United States is buying $6 worth of goods from China for every $1 worth of goods it ships to China. With American imports from China climbing at a clip of nearly 30 percent a year, American exports to China would have to nearly triple each year just to keep the deficit from widening further.

Many economists say that it is the United States' total trade deficit that is a more disturbing reflection of overall American weakness in trade. But it is the bilateral deficit between China and America that sets off fires on both sides.

China's economy is galloping along just as a long series of America's weaknesses are combining to hurt American exports. With many of America's name brands made in China these days, from clothing to cars, the Chinese are beginning to wonder what a "Made in U.S.A." label really has to offer. "The only U.S.-produced items that I can think of that exist in large quantities in China are dollar bills," said Matthew Crabbe, the managing director of Access Asia Ltd., a market research firm.

But the handful of products that Americans make well, and which sell like hotcakes, do not have labels on the sleeves—Boeing's aircraft and General Electric's power plant equipment, railway locomotive parts and aircraft engines. Beyond those, American exports to China consistently grow more slowly than imports, and [in 2005], they have slowed even more.

Regional Manufacturing in East Asia

To be sure, many economists question the value of focusing on any single bilateral trade deficit—even one that Rob Portman, the United States trade representative, decried in a speech in Beijing . . . as "the largest trade deficit in the history of the world."

Chinese officials increasingly try to deflect criticism by emphasizing America's growing dependence on borrowing from the world. That borrowing pays for a higher level of consumption than America's economic output would otherwise sustain. "Even if the United States stopped importing from China, it would have to buy from somewhere else," said Liao Xiaoqi, China's vice minister of commerce.

Another big reason for the expanding bilateral deficit lies in changing patterns of trade. Companies from Japan, South Korea, Taiwan and elsewhere in Asia increasingly manufacture only the most technologically sophisticated components at home. They ship them to China, buy the less complicated parts locally at low cost and assemble the product in China for shipment directly to Europe or the United States.

A result is that East Asia has achieved the dream that a dozen years ago gave rise to the North American Free Trade Agreement: a regional manufacturing center that taps each country for the part it can produce most efficiently.

The Influence of Free Trade

America's overall trade deficit with Asian countries has changed little in recent years, but the deficit is now concentrated in China.

The glue for this highly efficient regional export machine lies in the common rules of the World Trade Organization (W.T.O.), which China joined in November 2001. Those rules make it very hard for the United States, also a W.T.O. member, to impose limits on Chinese imports unilaterally, giving investors the confidence to put factories in China and to make use of the country's immense supply of cheap labor. Only in textiles and agriculture do W.T.O. rules allow more restrictions. The United States has limited Chinese textile exports; Chinese agricultural exports are small.

America's inability to sell to China is a result of many different limitations. A few of them are self-imposed, like American visa restrictions since the Sept. 11, 2001, attacks that make it harder for buyers to come to the United States, and limits on the export of technologies with potential military applications. "We are in essence restricting trade" by restricting visas, said David L. Cunningham Jr., the president of FedEx's Asia and Pacific division. "Business people take their business elsewhere."

Multinationals Building Factories in China

Other limits to American sales are a result of Chinese policies, like the Chinese government's purchase of $20 billion or more in dollars and other foreign currencies each month to prevent the Chinese currency from rising in value. China has also insisted that technology transfers to Chinese companies accompany any large import agreements for anything from cars to computer software.

That insistence, together with persistently low wages, has helped push multinationals to build, buy or invest in factories in China to supply the Chinese market, instead of exporting the same goods to it every year the way multinationals have long done in Africa, Latin America and elsewhere in Asia.

The Chinese market—a fifth of humanity—is so large that big corporations like General Motors (G.M.) and Caterpillar

The US Share of China's Goods Trade

% of China's Total Exports and Imports

Exports to US

Imports from US

SOURCE: China Customs and MBG Information Services.

have been much more willing to move production here than to other developing countries.

Even among Cadillacs, the top of G.M.'s line, G.M. now imports only the $150,000 Cadillac XLR sports car, which is manufactured at the same assembly plant in Bowling Green, Ky., that has long made the Chevrolet Corvette. G.M. has started building the Cadillac CTS sedan and Cadillac SRX car-based utility vehicle for the Chinese market in a 50-50 joint venture in Shanghai with the Shanghai Automotive Industry Corporation.

Caterpillar, based in Peoria, Ill., has been one of the most successful American companies in the Chinese market, but now relies heavily on factories in China to supply the market. "For Caterpillar and for every multinational, the key is to have a big presence in a country," said Richard P. Lavin, the company's vice president for Asian and Pacific operations.

The Resilience of American Agriculture

What China is buying, because it cannot grow or mine enough for itself, is food and minerals. American farmers—and the rural state lawmakers in Congress who represent them—have turned into a powerful lobby for free trade with China, as China erects few of the barriers that bedevil agriculture elsewhere. "We have not been told of any trade barriers for two years now, it's really amazing," said Phil Laney, the China director for the American Soybean Association.

Rejecting American Products

At the consumer level, tastes in China are also changing to the detriment of American companies. As China becomes increasingly cosmopolitan, an early admiration for all things American is fading. The generation of students who raised a copy of the Statue of Liberty during the Tiananmen Square protests in 1989 has gone on to acquire tastes as international as any in the world.

American car brands like Ford, marketed in the United States with a lot of waving flags, are promoted here as quality vehicles that show their owner's taste and sophistication. "Putting explicit American symbols in advertising will be alienating, not because of anti-Americanism but because of Chinese nationalism," said Tom Doctoroff, the chief executive for greater China at the JWT Advertising Agency.

Shopping at a store selling Coca-Cola merchandise in the same Tee Mall where Ms. Chan shopped, Estella Chong, an English teacher who has never lived outside China, said that attitudes had changed. "Maybe some people thought American brands were better than Chinese brands or had better after-sales service," she said. "Now they don't think so."

American Companies Lack Interest

Business hotels in China have a smattering of Americans and swarms of executives from China, the rest of Asia and often Europe, a sign of scant interest by small American companies.

The American Chamber of Commerce in Guangzhou in southeastern China helped organize an import opportunities fair here [in 2004] and arranged for American and Chinese officials to make presentations. But the heavily promoted event had to be canceled when fewer than a dozen American companies signed up to attend.

"American brands are not actively attacking the Chinese market—lazy, maybe," said Andrew Leung, a garment industry magnate who is the chairman of the Hong Kong Textile Council. "You see all the Italian brands doing quite well."

The Strength of American Innovation

The biggest strength of the United States in many markets has been its innovation. At a conference in Beijing [in November 2005], Gov. Arnold Schwarzenegger of California held up a new solar cell that had been designed in Silicon Valley, though it was actually manufactured in China.

But China's rampant copying of everything from movies to auto part designs makes it hard for American companies to profit even by licensing their ideas. The Chinese government is determined to move into higher-technology industries, moreover, and is hiring top scientists to be researchers. China wants new products to be "not just 'made in China' but 'designed in China,'" said Gov. Huang Huahua of Guangdong Province at a news conference. . . .

Decreasing the Cost of American Goods

Alan Greenspan, the [now former] chairman of the Federal Reserve, indicated . . . that a steep decline in the dollar was the most likely way that the overall American trade deficit would narrow, by making America's imports much more expensive, and American exports less costly overseas.

Ivy Chan, a 26-year-old secretary shopping at Tee Mall, said that she thought Motorola cellphones—an American brand partly designed in the United States and manufactured in China—were less attractive than Nokia phones. But a big drop in the price might make her reconsider. "I would buy it if it were a third cheaper," she said. "But I would think about why it is so cheap."

"To strengthen the [Israeli-Palestinian] cease-fire, existing official aid programs should continue."

The United States Should Continue Giving Aid to Palestine

David Aaron

David Aaron is director of the Rand Center for Middle East Public Policy. In the following viewpoint Aaron argues that cutting off aid to the Hamas-led Palestinian Authority (PA), the governing body of the Palestinians, would result in hunger, unemployment, and violence. He suggests continuing aid to Palestine as long as Hamas does not renew violent actions against its traditional enemy, Israel.

As you read, consider the following questions:

1. According to Aaron, what are the four risks of cutting off financial aid to Palestine, or replacing financial aid with humanitarian aid?

2. What does the author say the self-proclaimed priority of Hamas was following its election victory?

David Aaron, "How to Deal with Hamas," *Rand Corporation*, March 15, 2006. Copyright © 2006 by United Press International. Reproduced by permission.

3. Aaron suggests that new aid programs should be indefinitely postponed until Hamas does what?

After the surprise victory of Hamas in Palestinian elections [in January 2006], U.S. and European government policy remains dangerously obsolete and in disarray. To make the best of a bad situation will require a new approach based more on what Hamas does than on the hateful things it says.

Triggering Collapse by Cutting Off Government Aid

The United States and European Union nations are caught in the straight-jacket of their longstanding position: no contacts with Hamas (and hence no aid to the Palestinian Authority) until it renounces violence and recognizes Israel's right to exist as a Jewish state. Unfortunately, it is unrealistic to believe that Hamas will turn on a dime in the immediate aftermath of its election victory and publicly renounce its basic platform. This was demonstrated clearly in Hamas' [2006] meeting with the Russian government.

However, a cut-off in aid to the Hamas government could trigger the bankruptcy and collapse of the Palestinian Authority. This would create a chaotic and unpredictable situation of even greater unemployment, hunger and violence in Gaza and the West Bank. Israel would have to pick up the pieces by once again taking full control of Palestinian areas or live next to a failed state.

Humanitarian Aid Will Cause Problems

So the United States and its allies are scrambling to use "humanitarian aid" as a backdoor way to help the Palestinians. This cobbled-together strategy is likely to produce the worst of both worlds: it will create little incentive for Hamas to behave, yet carry all of the risks and costs the U.S. and Europe are trying to avoid.

First, the Palestinian Authority would still be strapped for cash and unlikely to avoid bankruptcy without turning to other Muslim states for desperately needed assistance. But the wealthy Arab countries have been notoriously stingy with the Palestinians in the past and are unlikely to open their checkbooks if this is opposed by the United States. So the cutoff in aid could well push the Palestinians into the arms of Iran—giving Iran a foothold on the Mediterranean and making it an even bigger threat to Israel, Europe and the United States.

Second, even if humanitarian programs continue, stopping all official aid would still damage America's democratization efforts in the Middle East. Rather than viewing the cutoff as a response to Hamas' inflammatory constitution, the Arab street would see it as punishing a freely elected government, thus further undermining U.S. credibility as a champion of democracy.

Third, the official aid cut-off would be an enormous gift to Hamas, which could place the onus for all its failures on the United States.

Finally, leaving all aid to humanitarian groups would mean governments might have little leverage to respond to unacceptable Hamas actions.

Compliance Should Yield More Aid

This is not an argument for business as usual. That would be seen as surrendering to terrorism. This would encourage more deadly terrorists attacks on the United States, Israel and throughout the region. It would be touted as a victory for jihad [the Muslim struggle against the infidels].

What then, is the alternative? The place to start is with Hamas' behavior. During the recent election campaign, Hamas declared and maintained a unilateral cease-fire with Israel. And since its victory, Hamas has indicated it does not plan to resume violence against Israel in the near future. Hamas lead-

Aid to Palestine Will Make the World Safer

If [the Palestinian leadership] continues to make promising overtures, the United States should next establish a major program of economic aid for the Palestinian people—one that matches the size of the substantial aid we give to Israel. We must make sure this assistance brings clear and immediate enhancement of Palestinian life—better health care, better schools. Where necessary, our help might extend to security systems—for example, running an airport in Gaza so people could fly in and out safely. We should put our money and our personnel where our public statements are. . . .

Can America afford such a program? If we help end the war between the Israelis and the Palestinians, we will actually save an extraordinary amount of money in the future—and live in a dramatically safer world.

Newt Gingrich, "Bolster the Peaceable Palestinians,"
American Enterprise, *April/May 2005.*

ers say that their immediate priority is building a Palestinian state and improving living conditions of the Palestinian people.

No one knows if this is true or just a ruse before stepped-up violence against Israel. But over time actions will speak louder than words. Giving Hamas incentives, both positive and negative, to maintain its cease-fire with Israel would buy time for Hamas to retreat from its stated goal of destroying Israel.

Pressure Historically Yields Limited Results

Arguments that this is a golden opportunity to put maximum pressure on Hamas to change its declared policy toward Israel need to be weighed against an historical fact. After decades of pressure, the late [Palestinian leader] Yasser Arafat and his Fatah organization finally used the right words in discussing Israel—ritually condemning terrorism and accepting the goal of Israel and Palestine living side by side in peace—but were never willing to turn the rhetoric into reality. Neither Arafat nor [his successor] President Mahmoud Abbas ever disarmed Hamas, Islamic Jihad, Fatah's own Al Aksa Martyrs Brigades and other terrorist organizations that have killed hundreds of Israelis and wounded thousands more.

What is worse? A Palestinian government that preaches peace but can't deliver it? Or a Palestinian government that stands for the destruction of Israel but just might maintain an indefinite cease-fire?

Seize the Opportunity

To strengthen the cease-fire, existing official aid programs should continue, but only so long as Hamas does not attack Israel and keeps other groups from doing so. The level of assistance should be calibrated to Hamas' actions, such as their relations with Iran. However, any new programs to support the Palestinian Authority should be held in abeyance until the Hamas government renounces terror and accepts the legitimacy of Israel.

The election of a Hamas government confronts the United States with fateful strategic choices rivaled only by the decision to go into Iraq. This is a period of grave risk and only a narrow opportunity. All concerned need to seize this opportunity to interrupt the cycle of violence, lest it be said of them what former Israeli Foreign Minister Abba Eban famously remarked about the Palestinians—that they "never miss an opportunity to miss an opportunity."

> *"The United States ... should refuse to fund a Palestinian regime that does not recognize the state of Israel and that actively supports the use of terrorism."*

The United States Should Cease Giving Aid to Palestine

Nile Gardiner and James Phillips

In the following viewpoint Nile Gardiner and James Phillips argue against providing economic aid to the Hamas-led government elected in Palestine because of Hamas's association with and support for terrorism. Gardiner and Phillips also suggest that if the United States provides any further aid to Palestine there must be greater disclosure as to how the money is spent to ensure that the money is not funding terrorist activities. Gardiner is director of the Margaret Thatcher Center for Freedom. Phillips is a research fellow in Middle Eastern affairs at the Heritage Foundation and is on the editorial board of Middle East Quarterly.

Nile Gardiner and James Phillips, "Congress Should Withhold Funds from the UN Relief and Works Agency for Palestine Refugees (UNRWA)," Heritage Foundation, February 6, 2006. www.heritage.org. Copyright © 2006 The Heritage Foundation. Reproduced by permission.

As you read, consider the following questions:

1. How does Rep. Ileana Ros-Lehtinen's bill categorize the Palestinian Authority and what does the bill call for, according to the authors?

2. Why do Gardiner and Phillips believe the United Nations Relief and Works Agency for Palestine Refugees in the Near East (UNRWA) is corrupt?

3. According to the authors, members of Congress led by Rep. Eliot Engel called on the U.S. government to pull funding for UNRWA until what condition was met?

The victory of Hamas in the [2006] Palestinian elections should force a wholesale reappraisal of U.S. and international funding for the Palestinian Authority (PA). Hamas is one of the most brutal and barbaric terrorist movements in modern history, being responsible for the murder of hundreds of Israeli, Palestinian, and American civilians and the maiming of thousands more. The United States and the European Union [EU] should refuse to fund a Palestinian regime that does not recognize the state of Israel and that actively supports the use of terrorism.

The U.S. and EU should also withhold all funding from the United Nations Relief and Works Agency for Palestine Refugees in the Near East (UNRWA) and call for an immediate inquiry into how it has been spending donors' money as well as allegations that it has hired members of terrorist organizations and stoked anti-Semitism among Palestinian refugees. Without this step, there is a major risk that a Hamas-led PA will exploit UNRWA to further its anti-Israel agenda.

Refusing to Fund Terrorist Agendas

The Palestinian Authority is hugely dependent upon foreign assistance, which accounts for about 66 percent of its annual budget. European Union funding for the PA amounted to $600 million in 2005. The United States gives $70 million directly to the PA each year, as well as $225 million for humanitarian projects through the U.S. Agency for International Development (USAID). Between 1993 and 2004, the Palestinian Authority received $6.93 billion in aid from the international community.

In addition to this direct funding of the PA, the U.S. and other nations give generously to UNRWA. In 2004, the U.S. pledged a total of $127 million. The U.S. provides roughly a quarter of UNRWA's regular annual budget and is the agency's biggest donor. The State Department's Bureau of Population, Refugees, and Migration has given over $300 million to UNRWA since 2001. According to the Palestinian Authority Ministry of Finance, UNRWA received an astonishing $3.95 billion in international funding between 1993 and 2004.

New legislation put forward in the House of Representatives by Rep. Ileana Ros-Lehtinen (R-FL) would de-fund the Palestinian Authority, an important step in the right direction. Her bill designates the PA as a "terrorist sanctuary" and would "prohibit direct assistance to the PA, the Palestinian Legislative Council, municipalities, and other constituent elements that are 'governed' by individuals associated with Hamas or other terrorist entities." Rep. Ros-Lehtinen's leadership on this issue sends a powerful signal from Capitol Hill that the United States will not allow its funds to be appropriated by terrorist groups.

Congress must also insist that international agencies that rely so heavily on U.S. funding and that will interact with the new Hamas regime be free of the taint of terrorist infiltration and operate in an accountable and transparent manner. Hamas has a long history of diverting funds from charitable organizations and abusing humanitarian fund-raising to support its terrorist agenda. It should not be allowed to subvert UNRWA or other groups to advance its radical Islamic goals.

The United States should send a clear message to UNRWA and other international bodies that their operations in Hamas-held territory and Palestinian refugee camps outside the Palestinian territories will be subject to intense scrutiny. In light of the Hamas election win, Congress and the [George W.] Bush Administration should withhold U.S. funding for UNRWA while the agency's finances are audited and alleged links between the agency and Hamas terrorists are thoroughly investigated. Washington must make every effort to ensure that taxpayer money is not being used for terrorist operations or political purposes. To this end, the amended 1961 Foreign Assistance Act directs that:

> No contributions by the United States should be made to [UNRWA] except on the condition that [UNRWA] take all possible measures to assure that no part of the United States contribution shall be used to furnish assistance to any refugee who is receiving military training as a member of the so-called Palestine Liberation Army or any other guerrilla type organization or who has engaged in any act of terrorism.

In addition to withholding funds, the United States should also state publicly that UNRWA, founded in 1949, is a costly anachronism that must be shut down in the near future, leaving its operations to the United Nations High Commissioner for Refugees (UNHCR). It is striking that UNRWA, with a staff of 24,300, had a regular budget in 2005 of $339 million to support 4.1 million refugees in just five territories (or $83 per refugee), while UNHCR, with a staff of 6,450, had a 2005 regular budget of $992 million to support 19.2 million refugees and asylum seekers in 116 countries (or $52 per refugee). UNRWA cannot justify its long-term existence as a separate entity on grounds of fairness, cost, or efficiency.

UNRWA Is a Corrupt Agency

Like most UN agencies, UNRWA is subject to little external oversight and minimal public scrutiny. For an agency that receives over a third of a billion dollars in public funding every year, it is extraordinarily opaque. Its website provides few spe-

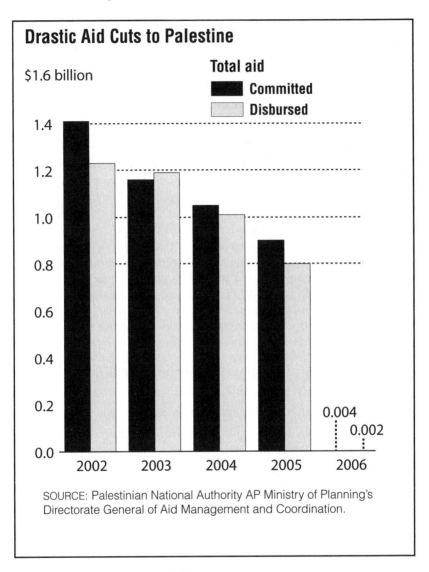

Drastic Aid Cuts to Palestine

$1.6 billion

Total aid
- Committed
- Disbursed

1.4
1.2
1.0
0.8
0.6
0.4
0.2
0.0

2002   2003   2004   2005   2006

0.004
0.002

SOURCE: Palestinian National Authority AP Ministry of Planning's Directorate General of Aid Management and Coordination.

cific details as to where the money goes and how it is spent. The agency is not externally or publicly audited. This is particularly troubling for an organization that has been so dogged by controversy.

There are serious allegations that UNRWA has been infiltrated by Hamas terrorists. According to the U.S. Government Account[ing] Office (GAO), as of November 2003 at least 16

UNRWA staff [members] had been detained by Israeli authorities for security-related crimes, and three had been convicted in military courts of terrorism-related activities.

UNRWA's leadership has admitted in the past that Hamas has people working inside the UN agency. Peter Hansen, then-Commissioner-General of UNRWA, sparked a political storm in 2004 when he remarked in an interview with the Canadian Broadcasting Corporation: "I am sure that there are Hamas members on the UNRWA payroll, and I don't see that as a crime. Hamas, as a political organization, does not mean that every member is a militant, and we do not do political vetting and exclude people from one persuasion as against another." (Hansen left the agency in March 2005 and was replaced by Karen Koning Abuzayd.)

Following Hansen's remarks, a bipartisan group of 37 Members of Congress led by Representative Eliot Engel (D-NY) called on the U.S. government to pull funding for UNRWA "until all members of terrorist organizations are removed from the Agency's staff." In a letter to then–Secretary of State Colin Powell, the Members noted: "[N]ot only have many of the suicide bombers of Hamas and other Palestinian terror organizations come from UNRWA refugee camps, but students in UNRWA schools have received a steady diet of hatred and anti-Semitism in their textbooks. Furthermore, reports widely indicate that terrorists have taken advantage of the limited restrictions Israel places on humanitarian vehicles, including the use of ambulances and other UN vans for illicit purposes."

That letter is no less relevant today, especially in light of Hamas's election win. Congress must increase its pressure on UNRWA funding, and the Bush Administration should use that threat to push for immediate reform and improved oversight of one of the UN's biggest agencies. . . .

No Money for Terrorists

As a major UN body with a huge budget, the United Nations Relief and Works Agency for Palestine Refugees should operate in a transparent and accountable manner. It must also remain politically neutral and must not aid terrorist groups and their supporters. There is a real danger that Hamas will exploit UNRWA as a lucrative cash cow to advance its anti-Israeli agenda.

Until it can be absolutely verified that UNRWA is being run in an effective, neutral, and accountable manner and that it will not be used by the new Hamas regime to pursue terrorism or spread anti-Semitism, the United States should withhold funds from the organization.

With the impetus from Congress, the Bush Administration should state clearly that UNRWA's operations must ultimately be taken over by UNHCR and that UNRWA should cease to exist as an independent agency within a few years.

Periodical Bibliography

The following articles have been selected to supplement the diverse views presented in this chapter.

Kristen Millares Bolt   "Starbucks Adjusts Its Formula in China," *Seattle Post-Intelligencer*, June 16, 2005.

Economist   "A Choosier Approach to Aid," April 23, 2005.

Peter L. Fitzgerald   "Tightening the Screws," *National Interest*, Winter 2001.

Delinda C. Hanley   "U.S. Aid to Palestinians Vital to Repair Effects of U.S. Aid to Israel," *Washington Report on Middle East Affairs*, April 2006.

Stephen P. Heyneman   "Are We Our Brothers' Keepers?" *World and I*, June 2003.

Henry J. Hyde   "Why Saying 'No' Counts," *Washington Times*, June 30, 2006.

Neil King Jr., Marc Champion, and Bill Spindle   "The Palestinian-Aid Puzzle," *Wall Street Journal*, March 27, 2006.

Jim Kouri   "U.S. Should Cut Off Aid to Palestinian Thieves," *American Chronicle*, January 29, 2006.

Joshua Kurlantzick   "Bush's Fake Aid," *Rolling Stone*, March 23, 2006.

Carlos Lozada   "Foreign Aid: Who Gets It and Why," *Commonweal*, May 17, 2002.

E. Anthony Wayne   "U.S. Foreign Policy: The Growing Role of Economics," *DISAM Journal*, Spring 2002.

Fareed Zakaria   "How to Change Ugly Regimes," *Newsweek*, June 27, 2005.

CHAPTER 4

What Is the
Global Impact of
American Culture?

Chapter Preface

Music is a cultural hallmark for every society throughout the globe. Each country has indigenous music styling that embodies the tastes and values of its people. These traditions are passed through generations and emended by imported sounds that result from intercultural contacts. In a rapidly globalizing world, however, some critics are concerned that waves of foreign influences are no longer being slowly incorporated into regional music styles but instead are quickly degrading them.

The chief culprit in these claims of musical degradation is American pop music. However, not every music critic foresees a homogenization of global music. Many experts point to the eclectic blend of influences that have combined to create the diverse scope of music produced in the United States. From African rhythms to Celtic folk songs to Indian sitar music, a wide range of foreign styles and instruments have permeated music made in America. Promoting this music around the world merely provides a means for further cross-cultural exchange.

Furthermore, according to some analysts, the eclectic nature of American music—including American pop music—has the capability of focusing attention on its foreign borrowings. For example, in *Technology Review* magazine, Henry Jenkins writes of how an American pop singer like Madonna can open up the market for Indian artists by incorporating bhangra, an Indian-inflected dance music, into a song like "Ray of Light." Music, then, becomes a site for cultural exchange not cultural imperialism.

In the following chapter authors debate the global influence of other types of American cultural products. From promoting American values and lifestyle to bridging cultural divides, American culture exports offer an unparalleled opportunity to communicate with the world—for better or worse.

> *"Many cultures around the world are gradually disappearing due to the overwhelming influence of corporate and cultural America."*

Cultural Globalization Is Americanized

Julia Galeota

Julia Galeota was seventeen years old when she wrote the following viewpoint, an essay that won a contest sponsored by the Humanist *magazine. In the viewpoint Galeota argues that American culture and cultural products dominate the globe. She claims that successful marketing campaigns have ensured that American trends—in movies, music, fashion, and other cultural venues—are dictating foreign consumers' tastes. In addition, news media and the Internet are barraging the world with images of America and its commercial brands. Galeota believes this cultural imperialism is subversive, but she is hopeful that not all countries are passively resigned to see their native cultures overwhelmed by a homogenized global culture of American design.*

As you read, consider the following questions:

1. In Galeota's view, what are the motivations behind American cultural imperialism?

Julia Galeota, "Cultural Imperialism: An American Tradition," *The Humanist*, vol. 64, May-June 2004, pp. 22-25. Copyright 2004 by The American Humanist Association. Reproduced by permission.

2. What new concept does the author say is driving U.S. corporate advertising strategies aimed at expanding global markets?

3. According to Galeota, what does David Rothkopf believe is the advantage of U.S. cultural imperialism?

Travel almost anywhere in the world today and whether you suffer from habitual Big Mac cravings or cringe at the thought of missing the newest episode of MTV's *The Real World* your American tastes can be satisfied practically everywhere. This proliferation of American products across the globe is more than mere accident. As a by-product of globalization, it is part of a larger trend in the conscious dissemination of American attitudes and values that is often referred to as *cultural imperialism*. In his 1976 work *Communication and Cultural Domination*, Herbert Schiller defines cultural imperialism as:

> the sum of the processes by which a society is brought into the modern world system, and how its dominating stratum is attracted, pressured, forced, and sometimes bribed into shaping social institutions to correspond to, or even to promote, the values and structures of the dominant center of the system.

Thus, cultural imperialism involves much more than simple consumer goods; it involves the dissemination of ostensibly American principles, such as freedom and democracy. Though this process might sound appealing on the surface, it masks a frightening truth: many cultures around the world are gradually disappearing due to the overwhelming influence of corporate and cultural America.

Spreading Culture Through Marketing

The motivations behind American cultural imperialism parallel the justifications for U.S. imperialism throughout history: the desire for access to foreign markets and the belief in the superiority of American culture. Though the United States does boast the world's largest, most powerful economy, no business is completely satisfied with controlling only the American market; American corporations want to control the other 95 percent of the world's consumers as well. Many industries are incredibly successful in that venture. According to the [Manchester, UK] *Guardian*, American films accounted for approximately 80 percent of global box office revenue in January 2003. And who can forget good old Micky D's? With over 30,000 restaurants in over one hundred countries, the ubiquitous golden arches of McDonald's are now, according to Eric Schlosser's *Fast Food Nation*, "more widely recognized than the Christian cross." Such American domination inevitably hurts local markets, as the majority of foreign industries are unable to compete with the economic strength of U.S. industry. Because it serves American economic interests, corporations conveniently ignore the detrimental impact of American control of foreign markets. . . .

It is easy enough to convince Americans of the superiority of their culture, but how does one convince the rest of the world of the superiority of American culture? The answer is simple: marketing. Whether attempting to sell an item, a brand, or an entire culture, marketers have always been able to successfully associate American products with modernity in the minds of consumers worldwide. While corporations seem to simply sell Nike shoes or Gap jeans (both, ironically, manufactured *outside* of the United States), they are also selling the image of America as the land of "cool." This indissoluble association causes consumers all over the globe to clamor ceaselessly for the same American products.

Selling Diversity

[In 1984], in his essay "The Globalization of Markets," Harvard business professor Theodore Levitt declared, "The world's needs and desires have been irrevocably homogenized." Levitt held that corporations that were willing to bend to local tastes and habits were inevitably doomed to failure. He drew a distinction between weak multinational corporations that operate differently in each country and strong global corporations that handle an entire world of business with the same agenda.

In recent years, American corporations have developed an even more successful global strategy: instead of advertising American conformity with blonde-haired, blue-eyed, stereotypical Americans, they pitch diversity. These campaigns— such as McDonald's new international "I'm lovin' it" campaign—work by drawing on the United States' history as an ethnically integrated nation composed of essentially every culture in the world. An early example of this global marketing tactic was found in a Coca Cola commercial from 1971 featuring children from many different countries innocently singing, "I'd like to teach the world to sing in perfect harmony/I'd like to buy the world a Coke to keep it company." This commercial illustrates an attempt to portray a U.S. goods as a product capable of transcending political, ethnic, religious, social, and economic differences to unite the world. (According to the Coca-Cola Company, we can achieve world peace through consumerism.)

More recently, Viacom's MTV has successfully adapted this strategy by integrating many different Americanized cultures into one unbelievably influential American network (with over 280 million subscribers worldwide). According to a 1996 "New World Teen Study" conducted by [advertising agency] DMB&B's BrainWaves division, of the 26,700 middle-class teens in forty-five countries surveyed, 85 percent watch MTV every day. These teens absorb what MTV intends to show as a diverse mix of cultural influences but is really nothing more than manufactured stars singing in English to appeal to American popular taste.

If the strength of these diverse "American" images is not powerful enough to move products, American corporations also appropriate local cultures into their advertising abroad. Unlike Levitt's weak multinationals, these corporations don't bend to local tastes; they merely insert indigenous celebrities or trends to present the facade of a customized advertisement. MTV has spawned over twenty networks specific to certain geographical areas such as Brazil and Japan. These specialized networks further spread the association between America and modernity under the pretense of catering to local taste. Similarly, commercials in India in 2000 featured Bollywood stars Hrithik Roshan promoting Coke and Shahrukh Khan promoting Pepsi. By using popular local icons in their advertisements, U.S. corporations successfully associate what is fashionable in local cultures with what is fashionable in America. America essentially samples the world's cultures, repackages them with the American trademark of materialism, and resells them to the world. . . .

News Media and Internet Outlets

Compounding the influence of commercial images are the media and information industries, which present both explicit and implicit messages about the very real military and economic hegemony of the United States. Ironically, the industry that claims to be the source for "fair and balanced" information plays a large role in the propagation of American influence around the world. The concentration of media ownership during the 1990s enabled both American and British media organizations to gain control of the majority of the world's news services. Satellites allow over 150 million households in approximately 212 countries and territories worldwide to subscribe to CNN, a member of Time Warner, the world's largest media conglomerate. In the words of British sociologist Jeremy Tunstall, "When a government allows news importation, it is in effect importing a piece of another country's politics—which is true of no other import." In addition to politics and commercials, networks like CNN also

present foreign countries with unabashed accounts of the military and economic superiority of the United States.

The Internet acts as another vehicle for the worldwide propagation of American influence. Interestingly, some commentators cite the new "information economy" as proof that American cultural imperialism is in decline. They argue that the global accessibility of this decentralized medium has decreased the relevance of the "core and periphery" theory of global influence. This theory describes an inherent imbalance in the primarily outward flow of information and influence from the stronger, more powerful "core" nations such as the United States. Additionally, such critics argue, unlike consumers of other types of media, Internet users must actively seek out information; users can consciously choose to avoid all messages of American culture. While these arguments are valid, they ignore their converse: if one so desires, anyone can access a wealth of information about American culture possibly unavailable through previous channels. Thus, the Internet can dramatically increase exposure to American culture for those who desire it.

Fear of the cultural upheaval that could result from this exposure to new information has driven governments in communist China and Cuba to strictly monitor and regulate their citizens' access to websites (these protectionist policies aren't totally effective, however, because they are difficult to implement and maintain). Paradoxically, limiting access to the Internet nearly ensures that countries will remain largely the recipients, rather than the contributors, of information on the Internet.

Resistance to Americanization

Not all social critics see the Americanization of the world as a negative phenomenon. Proponents of cultural imperialism, such as David Rothkopf, a former senior official in [President Bill] Clinton's Department of Commerce, argue that American cultural imperialism is in the interest not only of the United States but also of the world at large. Rothkopf cites Samuel Huntington's theory from *The Clash of Civilizations and the Beginning of the World Order*[1] that, the greater the cultural disparities in the world, the more likely it is that conflict will

1. The correct title of Huntington's book is *The Clash of Civilizations and the Remaking of the World Order*—The Editors.

occur. Rothkopf argues that the removal of cultural barriers through U.S. cultural imperialism will promote a more stable world, one in which American culture reigns supreme as "the most just, the most tolerant, the most willing to constantly reassess and improve itself, and the best model for the future." Rothkopf is correct in one sense: Americans are on the way to establishing a global society with minimal cultural barriers. However, one must question whether this projected society is truly beneficial for all involved. Is it worth sacrificing countless indigenous cultures for the unlikely promise of a world without conflict?

Around the world, the answer is an overwhelming "No!" Disregarding the fact that a world of homogenized culture would not necessarily guarantee a world without conflict, the complex fabric of diverse cultures around the world is a fundamental and indispensable basis of humanity. Throughout the course of human existence, millions have died to preserve their indigenous culture. It is a fundamental right of humanity to be allowed to preserve the mental, physical, intellectual, and creative aspects of one's society. A single "global culture" would be nothing more than a shallow, artificial "culture" of materialism reliant on technology. Thankfully, it would be nearly impossible to create one bland culture in a world of over six billion people. And nor should we want to. Contrary to Rothkopf's (and George W. Bush's) belief that, "Good and evil, better and worse coexist in this world," there are no such absolutes in this world. The United States should not be able to relentlessly force other nations to accept its definition of what is "good" and "just" or even "modern."

Fortunately, many victims of American cultural imperialism aren't blind to the subversion of their cultures. Unfortunately, these nations are often too weak to fight the strength of the United States and subsequently to preserve their native cultures. Some countries—such as France, China, Cuba, Canada, and Iran—have attempted to quell America's cultural influence by limiting or prohibiting access to American cultural programming through satellites and the Internet. However, according to the UN Universal Declaration of Human Rights, it is a basic right of all people to "seek, receive, and impart information and ideas through any media and regardless of frontiers." Governments shouldn't have to restrict their citizens' access to information in order to preserve their native cultures. We as a world must find ways to defend local cultures in a manner that does not compromise the rights of indigenous people.

> *"The conception of a harmonious and distinctively American culture—encircling the globe, implanting its values in foreign minds—has always been a myth."*

Cultural Globalization Is Not Americanized

Richard Pells

In the following viewpoint Richard Pells, a history professor at the University of Texas at Austin, argues that cultural globalization is not dominated by American tastes. Rather, as he explains, music, movies, cuisine, and other cultural elements from around the world have influence in a global society. Thus, in his view, America has been a recipient as well as a contributor to an ever-changing global culture. Furthermore, Pells maintains that the international community is not a passive receiver of American culture; people in all nations have the ability to shape their own preferences and commonly blend foreign influences with local traditions to create hybrids that suit their own tastes.

As you read, consider the following questions:

1. In Pells's view, why has America's culture spread so easily throughout the world?

Richard Pells, "From Modernism to the Movies: The Globalization of American Culture in the Twentieth Century," *European Journal of American Culture*, vol. 23, no. 2, 2004. Copyright © 2004 Intellect Ltd. Reproduced by permission.

2. What does the author mean when he says, "Sometimes
. . . a hamburger is just a hamburger"?

3. According to Pells, what other influences give people
throughout the world the ability to "resist" or "reinterpret" mass culture?

When people in other countries worried in the past, as
they do in the present, about the international impact
of American culture, they were not thinking of America's literature, painting, or ballet. 'Americanization' has always meant
the worldwide invasion of American movies, jazz, rock and
roll, mass-circulation magazines, best-selling books, advertising, comic strips, theme parks, shopping malls, fast food, television programmes, and now the Internet. This is, in the eyes
of many foreigners, a culture created not for patricians but for
the common folk. Indeed, it inspired a revolution in the way
we conceive of culture.

More recently, globalization has become the main enemy
for academics, journalists, and political activists who loathe
what they see as the trend toward cultural uniformity. Still,
they typically regard global culture and American culture as
synonymous. And they continue to insist that Hollywood,
McDonald's, and Disneyland are eradicating regional and local
eccentricities—disseminating images and subliminal messages
so beguiling as to drown out the competing voices in other
lands.

Reciprocal Cultural Exchange

Despite these allegations, the cultural relationship between the
United States and the world over the past 100 years has never
been one-sided. On the contrary, the United States was, and
continues to be, as much a consumer of foreign intellectual
and artistic influences as it has been a shaper of the world's
entertainment and tastes. What I want to emphasize, therefore, is how *reciprocal* America's cultural connections with
other countries really are.

That is not an argument with which many foreigners (or even many Americans) would readily agree. The clichés about America's cultural 'imperialism' make it difficult for most people to recognize that modern global culture is hardly a monolithic entity foisted on the world by the American media. Neither is it easy for critics of Microsoft or AOL Time Warner to acknowledge that the conception of a harmonious and distinctively American culture—encircling the globe, implanting its values in foreign minds—has always been a myth.

Nevertheless, the United States has been a recipient as much as an exporter of global culture. Indeed, immigrants from Europe, Asia, Latin America, and increasingly the Middle East, as well as African-Americans and the thousands of refugee scholar and artists who fled [Adolf] Hitler in the 1930s, have played a crucial role in the development of American science, literature, movies, music, painting, architecture, fashion, and food.

It is precisely these foreign influences that have made America's culture so popular for so long in so many places. American culture spread throughout the world because it has habitually drawn on foreign styles and ideas. Americans have then reassembled and repackaged the cultural products they received from abroad, and retransmitted them to the rest of the planet. In effect, Americans have specialized in selling the fantasies and folklore of other people back to them. This is why a global mass culture has come to be identified, however simplistically, with the United States. . . .

Recasting European Modernism

In short, the familiar artifacts of American culture may not be all that 'American.' Americans, after all, did not invent fast food, amusement parks, or the movies. Before the Big Mac, there were fish-and-chips, *wurst* [German sausage] stands, and pizzas. Before Disneyland there was Copenhagen's Tivoli Gardens (which Walt Disney used as a prototype for his first theme park in Anaheim, a model later re-exported to Tokyo and Paris).

Nor can the roots of American popular culture be traced only to native entertainers like P.T. Barnum or Buffalo Bill. Its origins lay as well in the European modernist assault, in the opening years of the twentieth century, on nineteenth century literature, music, painting, and architecture—particularly in the modernists' refusal to honour the traditional boundaries between high and low culture. Modernism in the arts was improvisational, eclectic, and irreverent. These traits have also been characteristic of, but not peculiar to, mass culture. . . .

The artists of the early twentieth century shattered what seemed to them the artificial demarcation between different cultural forms. They also questioned the notion that culture was primarily a means of intellectual or moral improvement. They did so by valuing style and craftsmanship over philosophy, religion, or ideology. Hence, they deliberately called attention to language in their novels, to optics in their paintings, to the materials in and function of their architecture, to the structure of music instead of its melodies. . . .

Although modernism assaulted the conventions of nineteenth century high culture in Europe and Asia, it inadvertently accelerated the growth of mass culture in the United States. Indeed, Americans were already receptive to the blurring of cultural boundaries. In the nineteenth century, symphony orchestras in the United States often included band music in their programmes, while opera singers were asked to perform both Mozart and Stephen Foster.

So, for Americans in the twentieth century. Surrealism, with its dreamlike associations, easily lent itself to the wordplay and psychological symbolism of advertising, cartoons, and theme parks. Dadaism ridiculed the snobbery of elite cultural institutions, and reinforced instead an already-existing appetite (especially among the immigrant audiences in

An American in Europe Discusses the Recasting of U.S. Cultural Imports

Just because American TV shows, channels, or other pop cultural imports appear in another country doesn't mean that they appear just as they are in America. . . . In other words, MTV here [in Europe] isn't MTV in America. CNN here is not CNN in America. Looking at MTV in Europe is a "foreign" experience for an American. The music played is largely different, a lot of it coming from European and other sources around the world. Have you ever heard French rap? How about German fatalism-minimalism-metal? How about British techno-DJ mixes? How about music from India, Africa, and Japan? This is the rude awakening Americans find when they tune in to European MTV: that not all music is sung in English and much American music is not popular here at all. . . . Also, the video jockeys (VJs) are not American. They're thoroughly European, representing European cultures, clothing, trends, languages, and so forth. The ads are not American and often aren't in English. And all those fatuous American shows that MTV produces are rarely if ever shown here.

Marnie Carroll, "American Television in Europe:
Problematizing the Notion of Pop Cultural Hegemony,"
Bad Subjects: Political Education for Everyday Life,
October 2001. http://bad.eserver.org.

America) for 'low-class,' disreputable, movies and vaudeville shows. [Igor] Stravinsky's experiments with atonal (and thus unconventional and unmelodic) music validated the rhythmic innovations of jazz. Writers like Ernest Hemingway and John Dos Passos, detesting the rhetorical embellishments of nineteenth century prose and fascinated by the stylistic innovations of [James] Joyce and [Marcel] Proust (among other European masters), invented a terse and hard-boiled language, devoted to reproducing as authentically as possible the elemental qualities of personal experience. This laconic style became a model for modern journalism, detective fiction, and movie dialogue.

All of these trends provided the foundations for a genuinely new culture. But the new culture turned out to be neither modernist nor European. Instead, America transformed what was still an avant-garde and somewhat parochial project, appealing largely to the young and the rebellious in Western society, into a global enterprise. . . .

The Negligible Impact of American Culture Abroad

If Americans have mostly adopted and reshaped the artistic traditions of Europeans and others, if the cultural relationship between America and the rest of the world has not been as one-sided as foreigners usually insist, and if global entertainment is in fact an artistic and intellectual smorgasbord, are people outside the United States really losing respect for their native cultures?

There is no doubt that America's culture is visible everywhere. But the ubiquitous presence of Coca-Cola billboards and fast-food chains is only a superficial sign of America's global influence. None of this has affected how people actually live, shop, eat, think about the role of their governments, use their cities, or entertain themselves in neighborhood cafés or in the privacy of their homes.

In reality, the effect of America's culture and consumer goods has been more negligible than intellectuals, politicians, and parents worried about the malleability of their Nike-clad children are willing to admit. Eating a Big Mac, lining up for the newest Hollywood blockbuster, or going to Disneyland in Paris or Tokyo doesn't automatically mean that one has become either 'Americanized' or a compliant inhabitant of the global village. The purchase of a Chicago Bulls T-shirt by a

Brazilian adolescent or the decision of a German family to have dinner at the nearby Pizza Hut does not necessarily signify an embrace of the American or the global way of life. Sometimes, to paraphrase Freud, a hamburger is just a hamburger, not an instrument of cultural or ideological seduction.[1] And neither the movies nor the Internet compel people to wear the same clothes, listen to the same music, idolize the same screen heroes, speak the same language, or think the same thoughts.

Nor are audiences—either adolescent or adult—a collection of zombies, spellbound by the images transmitted by the global media. Intellectuals often overestimate the power of mass culture to manipulate the masses. People in America and abroad are affected not just by the media but by their genes, their childhoods, their parents, their spouses and friends, by their experiences at work and their problems at home. These varied influences enable people to resist or at least reinterpret the media's messages rather than silently submit. Hence, far from being docile, audiences have adapted global culture to their own tastes and traditions. . . .

Local Cultures Still Dominate

Moreover, the critics of the international media conglomerates may have misjudged the ability of national, regional, local and ethnic cultures to survive and even to flourish in an age of globalization. The growth of regionalism, for example, is reflected not only in the Islamic resistance to and even hatred of 'Western' values, but in the tendency of different countries to export their own culture to neighboring lands. Mexico and Brazil transmit their films and television soap operas to other countries in Latin America. Sweden remains the dominant culture in Scandinavia. Egyptian and Indian movies are popular in other parts of the Middle East and Central Asia. The

1. Austrian psychiatrist Sigmund Freud had once stated that the image of a cigar appearing in a dream was probably a phallic symbol; when asked what that meant for his own love of smoking cigars, he purportedly replied, "Sometimes a cigar is just a cigar."

Hong Kong film industry is a major force in the East Asian market. At the same time, Argentina can look to France, Brazil to Africa, Chile to Spain, Mexico to its indigenous Indian language and history, for cultural alternatives to the United States. . . .

Finally, the movie and television industries in other countries are starting once again to capture the attention of local audiences. German television viewers increasingly favour dramas and situation comedies made in Germany. In Poland, which was inundated with American movies after the collapse of the Communist regime in 1989, several locally-produced films have attracted more ticket buyers than did *Titanic* or *Star Wars: The Phantom Menace*.

Nonetheless, film-makers in Europe and Asia have justifiably grumbled since the 1970s that they cannot get their works shown in the United States. For this they blame Hollywood's monopoly on distribution, and the alleged loathing of American audiences for movies that are subtitled or dubbed. Yet some foreign language films—particularly in the past decade—have been surprisingly successful and influential in the United States. These include Italian movies like *Cinema Paradiso, Il Postino*, and *Life Is Beautiful; Run Lola Run*, which is the most successful German film ever released in America; and *Crouching Tiger, Hidden Dragon*, which was the first foreign language film since Ingmar Bergman's *Cries and Whispers* in 1973 to be nominated for an Oscar for best picture of the year. Meanwhile, box office receipts in the United States for French films (like *Amélie* and *Under the Sand*) reached $30 million in 2001, compared with just $6.8 million in 2000. The renewed popularity and profitabilily of foreign films among general audiences in the United States should remind us that it has never been just college students and elite film critics who admire works that come from abroad. . . .

In the end, neither foreigners nor Americans have been passive receptacles for Hollywood movies or MTV: we are all free to choose what to embrace and what to ignore. Recognizing this may enable people in the twenty-first century to live more comfortably in what is, for all the arguments about 'Americanization' and the fears of 'globalization', still a decidedly pluralistic world.

> *"Cultural globalization is far from a recipe for American dominance."*

The American Media Do Not Dominate Global Culture

Charles Paul Freund

In the following viewpoint Charles Paul Freund argues that American movies and television programs are not dominating global culture. He maintains that while once the U.S. media outlets ruled the majority of global markets, newer, foreign media syndicates are now successfully competing with America. He claims that American fare remains popular abroad but that foreign nations are more apt to watch what their homegrown film and television enterprises are showing. Charles Paul Freund is a senior editor for Reason *magazine.*

As you read, consider the following questions:

1. According to Suzanne Kapner, as quoted by Freund, why do foreign nations seem to prefer domestic television programming?

2. According to the author, why did foreign networks broadcast mainly American television shows in the 1980s?

Charles Paul Freund, "American Culture Is Not Dominating the Globe (We Aren't the World)," *Reason*, vol. 34, no. 10, March 2003, pp. 55-58. Copyright 2003 by Reason Foundation, 3415 S. Sepulveda Blvd., Suite 400, Los Angeles, CA 90034. www.reason .com. Reproduced by permission.

3. As cited by Freund, what geographical region does Shekhar Kapur think will dominate media markets in the coming decades?

In the mid-1990s, the well-known French filmmaker Claude Berri warned that without protection from American cultural exports, "European culture is finished." He had plenty of pessimistic company. In that era, French Culture Minister Jack Lang spoke in terms of America's irrepressible "cultural imperialism." The popularity of a work like *Jurassic Park* was identified as a "threat" to others' "national identity." Strict programming quotas were enacted to prevent U.S.-made TV shows from overwhelming foreign primetime.

Meanwhile, scholars such as Herbert Schiller had worked out theories explaining how the American political empire was founded on its expanding communications empire, and critics such as Ariel Dorfman were busy publicizing the poisonous imperialistic messages buried in the adventures of such despoilers as Donald Duck.

Today, similar jeremiads are blowing as strong as ever: The leading prophet of cultural doom these days is Benjamin R. Barber, an academic growing hoarse as he warns against the dull global "monoculture" he thinks is being imposed by American capitalism. . . . But mounting evidence suggests that all this fulmination has been entirely pointless, and that cultural pessimists have been as clueless about the processes shaping the world as were their social, economic, and political forebears.

The Appeal of Local Television Programming

In January [2003], for example, *The New York Times* ran a front-page story reporting that exported American TV programs had largely lost their appeal for overseas audiences. According to the *Times*, these shows "increasingly occupy fringe time slots on foreign networks," leaving the prime-time hours to locally made shows.

"Given the choice," wrote London-based reporter Suzanne Kapner, "foreign viewers often prefer homegrown shows that better reflect local tastes, cultures and historical events." The problem, it turns out, is that many foreign broadcasters had not been giving their viewers much choice.

Why not? Many foreign networks had been created in a wave of 1980s privatization and lacked the financial and creative resources to produce their own programming. For a while, the most effective way to fill their schedules was by purchasing shows, especially American-made series. But as U.S. producers continued to drive up the price of their products, the now more-experienced broadcasters opted to make their own programs.

In brief, the foreign broadcasters chose neither to whine about nor to spin theories about American culture but rather to compete with it. As of 2001, more than 70 percent of the most popular shows in 60 different countries were produced locally. There are still popular American shows on foreign TV sets (especially movies), but as one European broadcaster told the *Times*, "You cannot win a prime-time slot with an American show anymore."

Foreign Markets Feature Homegrown Films

An even more dramatic shift may be going on with theatrical films. In 2001 "business for American films overseas fell by 16 percent against local product," according to Indian filmmaker Shekhar Kapur. Writing [in] August [2002] in the British newspaper *The Guardian*, Kapur noted: "The biggest success in Japan [in 2001] was not an American film, it was a Japanese film. The biggest success in Germany was not an American film, it was a German film. The biggest success in Spain was not an American film, but a Spanish film. The same in France. In India, of course, it's always been like that."

Hollywood Looks Overseas for Growing Market

[In 2005] the Walt Disney Company entered into a joint venture to make its first Chinese-language film. . . . In January [2006], Twentieth Century Fox . . . scored a major hit in Brazil with the Portuguese-language body-switching comedy "If I Were You." Sony . . . is a leader in local-language production and is making films in India, Russia and Mexico in 2006. . . .

One reason the studios are looking overseas is because moviegoing abroad is growing at a faster clip than in the United States. In 2005, the worldwide box office tallied $23.24 billion, a decrease of 7.9 percent from 2004, but still a 46 percent increase since 2000, according to the Motion Picture Association of America. . . . By contrast, the American box office, which represented $8.99 billion, or 39 percent, of that $23.24 billion, has increased only 17 percent since 2000.

Laura M. Holson, "The Search for Hits at a Foreign Box Office,"
New York Times, April 3, 2006.

Kapur believes that "American culture has been able to dominate the world because it has had the biggest home market." But the growing commercial importance of Asia—China, India, Japan—along with the larger markets of the Mideast and North Africa will change that, he argues. In other words, cultural globalization is far from a recipe for American dominance; it is an opportunity for other cultures and markets to assert themselves.

Kapur suggests this is already happening in such low-prestige areas as beauty contests, where the Miss USAs have been giving way in the finals to the Miss Indias. But Kapur also expects it to happen in such high-prestige venues as international journalism, because much of the ad revenue and investment will come from Asia.

"In 15 years from now," he writes, "we won't be discussing the domination of the western media but the domination of the Chinese media, or the Asian media. Soon we will find that in order to make a hugely successful film, you have to match Tom Cruise with an Indian or a Chinese actor."

Kapur may be oversimplifying, but he is right about the effects of competition. It is the smart cultures who are competing with the U.S. Indeed, it is American producers who have lately been borrowing cultural ideas, just to stay competitive. "Reality TV," surely the most reviled—if popular— format now on American screens, comes from Europe.

> "American movies ... are the truly po-
> tent examples of our cultural imperial-
> ism."

The American Media Dominate Global Culture

Neal Gabler

Neal Gabler, a film critic and author of film histories, argues in the following viewpoint that American media is still a strong force around the world. Gabler contends that American televi-sion—though once popular overseas—is giving way to local overseas programming, but American movies still dominate glo-bal markets. Gabler asserts that this is because U.S. television has a narrow, Americanized appeal while U.S. films still proffer universal themes.

As you read, consider the following questions:

1. As Gabler notes, what percentage of the world's gross film revenues do American movies account for?

2. According to the author, why did a German friend of his not understand the American television show *ER*?

3. What does Gabler say are three of the appealing charac-
teristics of the American television shows that remain
popular in foreign markets?

Once again, we are told, America's cultural hegemony is
cracking. The latest proof: American television programs,
which had dominated prime-time viewing in Europe and Asia
for decades, are now being consigned to the late-night fringes
of the schedule.

One European TV executive was quoted as saying that you
can no longer win a prime-time slot with an American show.
In markets as diverse as Malaysia, France and Latin America,
where "Dallas" and "Baywatch" were once blockbusters, locally
produced soap operas and crime shows rule the ratings. Today, "C.S.I.," the top-rated show in this country, cannot attract
even 3 percent of the viewers in South Korea.

Explanations for the decline range from general anti-
American political sentiment to growing resentment of American cultural influence to the rising cost of American shows.
There is also the privatization of the old state-run networks,
which has resulted in increased competition and greater de-
mand for programs to fill expanded schedules, even as, paradoxically, the popularity of each individual show plummets.

American Movies Still Dominate

Still, one shouldn't mourn the end of American cultural domination quite yet. There will always be the movies. And the
truth is, American movies, not TV shows, are the truly potent
examples of our cultural imperialism.

Films are far more costly than television programs and
also face increased local competition, yet American movies
don't seem to be suffering a similar diminution in popularity—they continue to rake in nearly 80 percent of the film
industry's worldwide take. Even in France, where sensitivity to
alleged American bullying and belief in native cultural superi-

ority may be stronger than anywhere else in the world, Hollywood movies continue to account for 50 percent to 70 percent of box office receipts every year.

All of which leads one to suspect that the reason American television shows are losing popularity has less to do with resentments or economics than with fundamental differences between American television and American film. Movies are universal, TV is not.

In the United States, the film exhibition industry erupted in the early 1900's in working-class urban neighborhoods and movies were regarded, in the words of *The Nation* magazine in 1913, as a "democratic art" intended specifically for the masses.

By the 1920's, however, film became the medium of the middle, cutting a wide swath through every demographic group. The studios, which owned the theaters, had made a concerted effort to broaden their films' appeal—making them longer and better, using marketing to establish the first heartthrobs and sirens, and erecting lavish movie palaces that would elevate the movie-going experience. By decade's end, 90 million Americans were attending the movies each week, three attendees for each American household.

The Broader Appeal of Hollywood's Exports

It was the ability of the movies to appeal to people of all ages, religions, ethnicities and regions that enabled Hollywood to export them. Already by 1925, 30 percent of the studios' profits came from overseas. (Today it is around 60 percent.) Part of this universality was aesthetic. Even after the silent era ended, the scale of American films, their speed and their action made them accessible to anyone.

Part of the attraction was ideological. American films, concentrating on stars framed in close-ups, promoted the centrality and the efficacy of individual action—a world that conformed to our vicarious will. Taken together, the artistry and the values made moviegoing an otherworldly experience. Movies may be the medium of the middle in the composition of their audiences, but they are the medium of the exceptional in the way they grab those audiences.

Though television arrived in this country in the late 1940's amid fears in Hollywood that it would usurp film's audience, those concerns obviously proved ungrounded. Television couldn't have been a more different medium. Whereas the movies were made to mesmerize hundreds gathered in the dark, television was pitched to families huddled in their living rooms and dens. Whereas the movies emphasized the extraordinary, television relied on the familiar.

From its inception, television was a medium not of the intrepid or the glamorous individual but of ensembles, and it required an understanding of group dynamics that was not always easily translatable to other cultures. A German colleague of mine told me that "ER" is virtually unintelligible (and unwatched) in his country because Germans don't understand the easy camaraderie between different races and classes on the show.

To this aesthetic barrier was added a sociological one. Since it was sponsor-supported, television pitched itself to clusters of viewers—potential buyers—rather than to the undifferentiated mass. It tried to attract what one might call a vertical audience rather than the large horizontal audience for which the movies aimed.

The "Clubbiness" of American Television

While Hollywood didn't tailor its product to blacks or Catholics or children, television always has. In its early days there was "The Goldbergs," about a Jewish family living in a Bronx tenement, "Beulah," starring Ethel Waters as a black maid, and "Life Is Worth Living," a prime-time religious program featuring Bishop Fulton Sheen. (Although there is more of a niche

America Makes, the World Takes

Everything the American industry makes, it makes not for "the market" but for one or another specific segment of a market that is global, growing like mad, and ever fractioning into submarkets. There is no such thing as American taste—there is the 27 percent of the population that goes to the movies at least once a month, but there is also the 30 percent that never goes to the movies. There is the under-thirty market, whose sensibilities dictate content . . . But wait—this group is increasingly losing in importance to the foreign market, whose sensibilities increasingly dominate . . . But wait—there is no one foreign market; there are ten major ones, and they have different tastes too. . . . America makes, the world takes—and America makes what the world wants to take.

Michael Kelly, "The Taste Business:
What Foreigners Love to Hate About America Is Also
What They Love to Buy,"
Atlantic Monthly, *July/August 2002.*

market in movies these days, no studio depends on movies of, say, black interest or religious appeal to hold up the bottom line.)

Television now reaches almost every household in America, but it has never lost its narrowcast mindset. It is still demographically driven, with programs aimed at slices of the audience. The result is that television has a kind of clubbiness, using references, gestures and attitudes that don't always cross our country's demographic lines, much less international borders.

Indeed, the American shows that have traveled best around the globe are those that deal in the basics—sex ("Baywatch") and melodrama ("Dallas")—and even with these shows part of the appeal for foreign markets was that they reinforced the stereotype of American vulgarity.

The decline of American shows around the world, then, should be seen as a fulfillment of television's destiny, a destiny that had only been postponed until local markets gained the know-how, the money and the corporate structure to make their own programs for slices of their own audience. It also reflects a technological advance—the new panoply of cable and satellite channels that are breaking TV audiences down into niche groups—that perfectly mirrors what has been happening in America for the last three decades.

Our movies continue to be universal, exporting the primal aesthetic of excitement and individualism. Our TV shows continue to be domestic. And the rest of world is likely to continue to be divided between the American movies they love and the American television shows they don't really understand and, more and more, don't really care to watch.

> *"America is ... exporting more than enough depictions of profanity, nudity, violence and criminal activity to violate norms of propriety still honored in much of the world."*

America's Pop Culture Exports Are Damaging the Nation's Image

Martha Bayles

Martha Bayles, formerly a television and arts critic for the Wall Street Journal, *now teaches humanities at Boston College. In the following viewpoint Bayles argues that American pop culture exports give the rest of the world a negative view of Americans. She notes that the violence and coarseness displayed in American music, television, and films is often the only image of Americans that many foreigners encounter. She contends that if pop culture is a form of political propaganda, then the United States is not winning any friends overseas.*

Martha Bayles, "Now Showing: The Good, the Bad and the Ugly Americans: Exporting the Wrong Picture," *Washington Post*, August 28, 2005, p. B01. Copyright © 2005 the *Washington Post*. Reproduced with permission of the author.

As you read, consider the following questions:

1. As Bayles writes, why do we, as Americans, "still seem to congratulate ourselves that our popular culture now pervades just about every society on Earth"?

2. According to the author, what happens to offensive lyrics in songs played on Radio Sawa?

3. Why does Bayles say that censoring American pop culture exports "is not the answer"?

When Benjamin Franklin went to France in 1776, his assignment was to manipulate the French into supporting the American war for independence. This he accomplished with two stratagems: First, he played the balance-of-power game as deftly as any European diplomat; and second, he waged a subtle but effective campaign of what we now call public diplomacy, or the use of information and culture to foster goodwill toward the nation. For Franklin, this meant turning his dumpy self into a symbol. "He knew that America had a unique and powerful meaning for the enlightened reformers of France," writes historian Bernard Bailyn, "and that he himself . . . was the embodiment, the palpable expression, of that meaning." Hence the fur cap and rustic manner that made Franklin a celebrity among the powdered wigs and gilded ornaments of the court of Louis XVI.

Today, as we witness the decline of America's reputation around the world, we're paying far more attention to Franklin's first stratagem than to his second. Indeed, despite a mounting stack of reports recommending drastic changes in the organization and funding of public diplomacy, very little of substance has been done. And most Americans, including many who make it their business to analyze public diplomacy, seem unmindful of the negative impression that America has recently been making on the rest of humanity—via our popular culture.

A Misguided View of Americans

A striking pattern has emerged since the end of the Cold War. On the one hand, funding for public diplomacy has been cut by more than 30 percent since 1989, the National Science Board reported [in 2004]. . . . On the other hand, while Washington was shrinking its funding for cultural diplomacy, Hollywood was aggressively expanding its exports. The Yale Center for the Study of Globalization reports that between 1986 and 2000 the fees generated by the export of filmed and taped entertainment went from $1.68 billion to $8.85 billion—an increase of 427 percent. Foreign box-office revenue has grown faster than domestic, and now approaches a 2-to-1 ratio. The pattern is similar for music, TV and video games.

This massive export of popular culture has been accompanied by domestic worries about its increasingly coarse and violent tone—worries that now go beyond the polarized debates of the pre-9/11 culture war. For example, a number of prominent African Americans, such as Bill Stephney, cofounder of the rap group Public Enemy, have raised concerns about the normalization of crime and prostitution in gangsta and "crunk" rap. And in April 2005, the Pew Research Center reported that "roughly six-in-ten [Americans] say they are very concerned over what children see or hear on TV (61%), in music lyrics (61%), video games (60%) and movies (56%)."

These worries now have a global dimension. The 2003 report of the U.S. House of Representatives Advisory Group on Public Diplomacy for the Arab and Muslim World stated that "Arabs and Muslims are . . . bombarded with American sitcoms, violent films, and other entertainment, much of which distorts the perceptions of viewers." The report made clear that what seems innocuous to Americans can cause problems abroad: "A Syrian teacher of English asked us plaintively for help in explaining American family life to her students. She asked, 'Does "Friends" show a typical family?'"

One of the few efforts to measure the impact of popular culture abroad was made by Louisiana State University researchers Melvin and Margaret DeFleur, who in 2003 polled teenagers in 12 countries: Saudi Arabia, Bahrain, South Korea, Mexico, China, Spain, Taiwan, Lebanon, Pakistan, Nigeria, Italy and Argentina. Their conclusion, while tentative, is nonetheless suggestive: "The depiction of Americans in media content as violent, of American women as sexually immoral and of many Americans engaging in criminal acts has brought many of these 1,313 youthful subjects to hold generally negative attitudes toward people who live in the United States."

The Decline of American Pop Culture

Popular culture is not a monolith, of course. Along with a lot of junk, the entertainment industry still produces films, musical recordings, even television shows that rise to the level of genuine art. The good (and bad) news is that censorship is a thing of the past, on both the producing and the consuming end of popular culture. Despite attempts by radical clerics in Iraq to clamp down on Western influences, pirated copies of American movies still make it onto the market there. If we go by box office figures, the most popular films in the world are blockbusters like "Harry Potter." But America is also exporting more than enough depictions of profanity, nudity, violence and criminal activity to violate norms of propriety still honored in much of the world.

But instead of questioning whether Americans should be super-sizing to others the same cultural diet that is giving us indigestion at home, we still seem to congratulate ourselves that our popular culture now pervades just about every society on Earth, including many that would rather keep it out. Why this disconnect? Partly it is due to an ingrained belief that what's good for show business is good for America's image. During both world wars, the movie studios produced propaganda for the government, in exchange for government aid in opening resistant foreign markets. Beginning in 1939, the recording industry cooperated with the Armed Forces Network to beam jazz to American soldiers overseas, and during the Cold War it helped the Voice of America (VOA) do the same for 30 million listeners behind the Iron Curtain.

In his book, *Cultural Exchange & the Cold War*, veteran foreign service officer Yale Richmond quotes the Russian novelist Vasily Aksyonov, for whom those VOA jazz broadcasts were "America's secret weapon number one." Aksyonov said that "the snatches of music and bits of information made for a kind of golden glow over the horizon . . . the West, the inaccessible but oh so desirable West."

To my knowledge, this passage has not been quoted in defense of Radio Sawa, the flagship of the U.S. government's new fleet of broadcast channels aimed at reaching young, largely Arab audiences. But even if it were, who could imagine such a reverent, yearning listener in the Middle East, South Asia or anywhere else today? The difference is not just between short-wave radio and unlimited broadband, it is also between Duke Ellington and 50 Cent.

Pop Culture as Propaganda

During the Cold War, Washington also boosted the commercial export of popular culture, adhering to the view set forth in a 1948 State Department memo: "American motion pictures, as ambassadors of good will—at no cost to the American taxpayers—interpret the American way of life to all the nations of the world, which may be invaluable from a political, cultural, and commercial point of view."

And this boosterism continued through the 1960s and '70s, even as movies and rock music became not just unruly but downright adversarial. During the 1970s, the government worked so hard to pry open world markets to American entertainment that UNESCO [United Nations Educational, Scientific, and Cultural Organization] and the Soviet Union led a

Potential Dangers of Soft Power

The American victory in the soft war creates the desire of the citizens of the world to become American, with its values, wealth and security umbrella. However, it is impossible for America to grant the American dream to all people who dream it, either in the U.S. or abroad. The danger of creating a desire that cannot be satisfied—whether desire for a certain product or a certain civilization—is the backlash that will follow: waves of protest and dissatisfaction that will translate into a wish to return to one's own history.

This has repercussions within the U.S. too, as the country is composed of people coming from all over the world who will sympathize with their fellows outside America. We have an example here: some U.S. residents and citizens supported the al-Qaeda terrorists.

Francesco Sisci, "Risky Business: Exporting the American Dream,"
Asia Times Online, March 15, 2002. www.atimes.com.

backlash against "U.S. cultural imperialism." In 1967, the VOA began to broadcast rock and soul. And while a provocative figure like [avant-garde rock musician] Frank Zappa was hardly a favorite at diplomatic receptions, many in the foreign service understood his symbolic importance to dissidents, including Czech playwright (and later president) Vaclav Havel. In general, the U.S. political establishment was content to let America's homegrown counterculture do its subversive thing in Eastern Europe and Russia.

In the 1980s, the mood changed. Under [President] Ronald Reagan appointee Charles Z. Wick, the United States Information Agency (USIA), the autonomous agency set up in 1953 to disseminate information and handle cultural exchange, was more generously funded and invited to play a larger role in policymaking—but at the price of having its autonomy curbed and the firewall between cultural outreach and policy advocacy thinned. It is noteworthy that these changes occurred amid the acrimony of the culture wars. Like the National Endowment for the Arts and public broadcasting, the USIA eventually found itself on Sen. Jesse Helms's list of artsy agencies deserving of the budgetary ax. And while the others managed to survive, the USIA did not. In 1999 it was absorbed into the very different bureaucratic culture of the State Department.

Today we witness the outcome: an unwarranted dismissal of elite-oriented cultural diplomacy, combined with an unquestioned faith in the export of popular culture. These converge in the decision to devote the bulk of post-9/11 funding to Radio Sawa and the other commercial-style broadcast entities, such as al-Hurra (a U.S.-based satellite TV network aimed at Arab listeners) and Radio Farda (which is broadcast in Farsi to Iran). Because the establishment of these new channels has been accompanied by the termination of the VOA's Arabic service, critics have focused largely on their news components. But what benefit is there in Radio Sawa's heavy rotation of songs by sex kitten Britney Spears and foul-mouthed rapper Eminem?

To the charge that the [George W.] Bush administration is peddling smut and profanity to Arab teens, Radio Sawa's music director, Usama Farag, has stated that all the offensive lyrics are carefully edited out. Yet there is something quaint about the U.S. government's censoring song lyrics in a world where most people have ready access to every product of the American entertainment industry, including the dregs.

Make American Pop Culture a Positive Global Ambassador

American popular culture is no longer a beacon of freedom to huddled masses in closed societies. Instead, it's a glut on the market and, absent any countervailing cultural diplomacy, our de facto ambassador to the world. The solution to this problem is far from clear. Censorship is not the answer, because even if it were technologically possible to censor our cultural exports, it would not be politic. The United States must affirm the crucial importance of free speech in a world that has serious doubts about it, and the best way to do this is to show that freedom is self-correcting—that Americans have not only liberty but also a civilization worthy of liberty.

From Franklin's days, U.S. cultural diplomacy has had both an elite and a popular dimension. Needless to say, it has rarely been easy to achieve a perfect balance between the two. What we could do is try harder to convey what the USIA mandate used to call "a full and fair picture of the United States." But to succeed even a little, our new efforts must counter the negative self-portrait we are now exporting. Along with worrying about what popular culture is teaching our children about life, we need also to worry about what it is teaching the world about America.

"The world needs more MTV, McDonald's, Microsoft, Madonna, and Mickey Mouse."

America's Pop Culture Exports Are Spreading American Values

Matthew Fraser

Matthew Fraser is editor in chief for the Canadian National Post *newspaper and was formerly a professor at Ryerson University in Toronto. In the following viewpoint Fraser states that popular culture exports are part of American "soft power"—the nation's strategy to persuade other parts of the world to accept and embrace America's worldview. As such, spreading pop culture can aid the country diplomatically by promoting American values overseas. Fraser notes that this is a form of cultural imperialism, but to cease spreading U.S. values, he predicts, would be destructive to U.S. interests and destabilizing for the world.*

As you read, consider the following questions:

1. What does Fraser categorize as American soft power?

2. What has American soft power become in the post–Cold War era, according to the author?

3. In Fraser's view, how does American soft power help fight terrorism?

So, all things considered, do things really go better with Coca-Cola? Would the world be a better place if Disneyland theme parks were constructed in Baghdad [Iraq] and Damascus [Syria]? Would global stability be less precarious if Big Macs were sold with a smile in Pyongyang [North Korea] and Tehran [Iran]?

These questions . . . are not as facetious as they seem. And the easy answer is a resolute yes. Supported by historical analysis . . . , we persist in the affirmation that American soft power—movies, television, pop music, fast food—promotes values and beliefs that, while contentious, are ultimately good for the world. American entertainment—Hollywood, Disneyland, CNN, MTV, and Madonna—conveys values that have made America great, such as an abiding belief in democracy, free enterprise, and individual liberties. What's more, much of the world's population has embraced America as a model society that has championed these values. Whatever America's shortcomings, there are many more people seeking to emigrate to the United States than are actively engaged in Jihad [Muslim religious war] against it.

The values of American pop culture are penetrating even the most stubbornly resistant societies where despotic regimes rule with the iron fist of tyranny and oppression. In communist North Korea, Kim Jong-il idolizes Michael Jordan, and his eccentric heir Kim Long-nam is fascinated by Mickey Mouse. True, weapons of mass distraction cannot triumph over weapons of mass destruction. But they can temper the pernicious values and beliefs that build them.

Soft Power Is Part of U.S. Foreign Policy

The deployment of American soft power ... has played a role in U.S. foreign policy for nearly a century. From Woodrow Wilson to George W. Bush, the White House has been acutely aware of the strategic importance of pop culture as a powerful conveyor of American values and ideals throughout the world.... For most of the 20th century American soft power was marshalled to promote the national interests of the United States. Pop culture was, in effect, an extension of U.S. trade policy, which of course served the interests of American capitalism. At the same time, however, American soft power took inspiration from fundamental values commonly associated with the "American way." The Cold War brought those values into focus, and for nearly half a century U.S. soft power was driven by the dictates of geopolitical realism and the loftier goals of moral idealism. In the post–Cold War world, as America asserted its imperial ambitions, soft power has become an overarching frame of reference for the entire Western world bonded by common cultural values and strategic interests. It is not insignificant that the Golden Arches can be found nowhere in countries—Iraq, North Korea, Iran—whose regimes have been hostile to everything America represents. The absence of Golden Arches in certain countries tells us more about geopolitics than about gastronomical predilections.

Today, communications technologies such as the Internet and satellites have intensified the ubiquity, velocity, and impact of American soft power. Local cultures cannot build electronic Berlin Walls against foreign influences; if they do, they quickly discover that these ramparts are hopelessly porous. MTV's signals are beamed down from geostationary orbit, while CNN's Web site can be accessed on computers in virtually any country on the planet. In the Information Age, soft-power resources have become strategic resources and America's adversaries know this. For this reason, the threat of cyberter-

Foreign Audiences Can Distinguish Between Entertainment and Reality

I believe the world can clearly distinguish between entertainment and reality. I grew up in Pakistan and there were many who frowned on certain American shows and artists for nudity/language/promiscuity reasons. However, people also knew that was just entertainment and to this day what Pakistanis admire about the U.S. is the economy, legal system, tolerance and openness of American culture. Certainly cultural exports can create a good image for the country, but policies and the internal shape of a country are far more important than that.

Reader response to Martha Bayles,
"Outlook: Exporting American Popular Culture,"
Washington Post, *August 29, 2005. www.washingtonpost.com.*

rorism has become increasingly preoccupying in the United States, especially in the wake of [the terrorist group] Al Qaeda's attacks on the World Trade Center and Pentagon [in 2001]. . . .

Make no mistake, the American Empire is a military and economic superpower. The United States boasts a defence budget greater than the combined military spending by the next 14 nations. What's more, the American economy is three times larger than its four largest rivals—Japan, Germany, Britain, and France—combined. Given these awesome advantages, America is now regarded as a unipolar superpower with no likely rival in the foreseeable future. It has been our contention, however, that the American Empire, like all empires, is essentially a *cultural* construction. The role of American soft power consequently has been crucial to the extension and maintenance of American imperial power. . . .

The Importance of Keeping U.S. Values in Circulation

America is a benevolent hegemon, especially when compared with previous imperial powers. But what about the alleged dangers of American hegemony? So far, the only dangers are to America itself. The cost of maintaining a global empire is great, especially since America borrows more than it lends. True, there is a persistent claim that American soft power promotes a barren global monoculture, and anti-globalization protestors continue to denounce corporate America and rail against the World Trade Organization as the handmaiden of global capitalism. They can even find support among insurgent nationalists, like the anti-American demonstrators in Serbia who trashed a McDonald's in Belgrade and brandished placards shouting: "Stop NATO-Cola!" Some claim America, labelled as a global "brand bully," is undermining its own influence by aggressively promoting the expansion of Disney, Coca-Cola, and McDonald's. As *BusinessWeek* put it in a headline: "Cultural imperialism is no joke." Why? Because American imperialism could potentially backfire if other societies become unstable due to social and cultural ruptures produced by its effects. . . .

But how long can an American Empire endure? The Roman Empire collapsed, and so, in like manner, will the American Empire vanish some day. But that day is a long way off. Like the Roman Empire, the American Empire of the 21st century is both a formal imperial system and an informal empire of values and beliefs and meaning. Unlike the Roman Empire, the American Empire possesses the advantage of powerful communications technologies that export, distribute, and transmit cultural messages with awesome efficiency. Even the culturally proud French are increasingly Americanized. Following the shocking events of 9-11, the leftist Parisian newspaper *Le Monde* declared on behalf of France: "*Nous sommes tous Américains*"—we are all Americans.

We know that the Roman Empire fell after constant attacks from belligerent barbarians. Today, the American Empire, too, is similarly under attack. America's adversaries are terrorist cells motivated by fanatical ideals that are antithetical to Western values. Not surprisingly, these threats represent the most serious challenge to U.S. foreign policy. In the fight against terrorism, American soft-power resources have become important cultural antidotes to prevent the growth of attitudes and values that foment hatred and incite violence. It terrorism triumphs, our fate could be that of Rome—a collapse leading to a chaotic neo-medieval order with no central authority. America would become a latter-day Holy Roman Empire, struggling to contain violence and establish order in a world fraught with constant peril, disease, and disorder. At the dawn of the 21st century, there are already ominous signs of an emerging world overrun with private armies, terrorists, and drug cartels. The moats and drawbridges of the Middle Ages could well be replaced by a world order where the distinction between public and private property becomes blurred; where the centres of authority are uncertain; where Visigoths and Vandals are Islamic fundamentalists in hijacked jetliners; where, in short, the center cannot hold and frightening passions are unleashed upon the world. As [former U.S. national security adviser] Zbigniew Brzezinski puts it: "The only alternative to American power is global anarchy."

Given these hard realities, it is surprising that American cultural imperialism has been so persistently challenged as a destructive force. We have attempted to demonstrate that America's weapons of mass distraction are not only necessary for global stability, but also should be built up and deployed more assertively throughout the world. The world needs more MTV, McDonald's, Microsoft, Madonna, and Mickey Mouse.

Yes, things really do go better with Coke.

Periodical Bibliography

The following articles have been selected to supplement the diverse views presented in this chapter.

Kwame Anthony Appiah — "The Case for Contamination," *New York Times Magazine*, January 1, 2006.

Richard De Zoysa and Otto Newman — "Globalization, Soft Power and the Challenge of Hollywood," *Contemporary Politics*, September 2002.

Economist — "Puritans or Pornographers?" February 25, 2006.

Michael Hastings, Stefan Theil, and Dana Thomas — "The Deadly Noodle," *Newsweek International*, January 20, 2003.

Henry Jenkins — "Culture Goes Global," *Technology Review*, July/August 2001.

Clark S. Judge — "Hegemony of the Heart: American Cultural Power and Its Enemies," *Policy Review*, December 2001.

Anthony Kaufman — "Is Foreign Film the New Endangered Species?" *New York Times*, January 22, 2006.

Philippe Legrain — "In Defense of Globalization: Why Cultural Exchange Is Still an Overwhelming Force for Good," *International Economy*, Summer 2003.

Clay Risen — "Remaindered: The Decline of Brand America," *New Republic*, April 11, 2005.

G. Pascal Zachary — "The World Gets in Touch with Its Inner American," *Mother Jones*, January/February 1999.

Mortimer B. Zuckerman — "What Sets Us Apart," *U.S. News & World Report*, July 3, 2006.

For Further Discussion

Chapter 1

1. Many nations—both enemies and allies—have accused the United States of being a rogue superpower, especially since the collapse of the Soviet Union. Robert F. Drinan, for example, claims that the George W. Bush administration has reinforced this notion by withdrawing from the Kyoto Protocol on global warming and staging preemptive wars to suit U.S. interests. On the other hand, undersecretary of state for global affairs Paula J. Dobriansky maintains that much of what is mistakenly referred to as U.S. unilateralism is really evidence of U.S. leadership. Like other defenders of the administration's foreign policy, Dobriansky contends that America always seeks wide counsel before acting but cannot afford to remain idle when facing urgent international crises. Consider specifically the U.S. invasion of Iraq and the war on terror; do you think the United States has acted unilaterally or has the country taken a multilateral approach to these foreign policy issues? Explain your answer, citing from the viewpoints.

2. Part of what is referred to as the Bush Doctrine entails the president's commitment to spreading democracy throughout the globe. As Bush states in his viewpoint, the aim of spreading democracy is to end tyranny where it remains. Joseph T. Siegle and Morton H. Halperin, however, assert that the president's doctrine rings hollow because his administration has supported existing dictatorial regimes and has simply built its own form of tyranny in the proving grounds of Iraq and Afghanistan. After examining the arguments made in this pair of viewpoints, do you think the U.S. government is committed to bringing democracy to

the world? How effective has the United States been in spreading democracy? What do you believe are the goals of such an enterprise? Explain your answers.

Chapter 2

1. After reading the viewpoint by Nikolas K. Gvosdev and Paul J. Saunders and the viewpoint by William E. Odom, state your views on whether the United States should or should not pull out of Iraq. Discuss the compelling reasons that have influenced your decision. Also address what sacrifices the nation would be making in following your proposed course of action.

2. Alan Dershowitz concludes that Iraq was the wrong target for U.S. intervention because Saddam Hussein's empire, in Dershowitz's view, did not pose a credible threat to world peace. He instead argues that Iran is more of a danger to U.S. interests and Middle East security than Iraq ever was. Do you believe Dershowitz is correct in his opinion that the United States and its allies should have taken (or should still take) military action against Iran? Or do you believe, as Richard K. Betts does, that attacking Iran would be too politically, diplomatically, and strategically damaging to the United States? Consider the strengths and weaknesses of both authors' arguments when explaining your view.

3. Using examples and opinions from various articles in this chapter, explain how effective you think the U.S. war on terror has been. What are the benefits and consequences of conducting this war? Should any of the consequences affect the nation's pursuit of the war, or, as Condoleezza Rice implies, should America stick to a long-term strategy that history will prove correct? Explain your answer.

Chapter 3

1. The Millennium Challenge Account (MCA) and the Millennium Challenge Corporation (MCC) determine candidates for economic aid by rating the governments of candidate countries in three categories: economic policies, just rule, and investment in the people. Paul V. Applegarth asserts that this ratings system effectively assays which governments are best suited to distribute the aid and reduce poverty. Aldo Caliari argues, however, that the rating system used by the MCA is too subjective and unreliable. Do you think that the MCA provides objective guidelines for deciding which countries will receive economic aid or does it reward countries with governments most like that of the United States? Explain your answer.

2. Keith Bradsher asserts, through the testimony of numerous individuals, that American goods have only a minimal impact on the Chinese market. According to industry experts and Chinese consumers quoted by Bradsher, American products are less appealing than similar items made in Europe, China, and other parts of Asia. Jehangir S. Pocha, however, contends that Chinese consumers are eager to purchase American brand name items simply because they are American. Which author do you think makes a more convincing argument? Why?

3. Following the election of individuals affiliated with the extremist group Hamas to the Palestinian Authority (PA) in January 2006, the United States and its allies have debated over how much economic aid, if any, should be given to the PA. Nile Gardiner and James Phillips maintain that all funding to the PA should be cut because Hamas is a recognized terrorist organization that will use the money to fund anti-Israel and terrorist activities. David Aaron argues that if aid is no longer sent to the PA, new and more threatening scenarios could develop in the Middle East. Basing your answer on the arguments made

by these authors, do you think that the United States should continue to send economic aid to the PA or should aid to the PA be stopped? Cite examples from the articles to support your view.

Chapter 4

1. Julia Galeota argues that America has been actively selling its products, its image, and its values to the world in order to increase the nation's global influence. The resulting Americanized global culture, she contends, is adversely affecting native cultures in foreign lands. Richard Pells, however, believes that foreign populations are strong enough to resist Americanization and merely take from American culture what they find appealing. Whose argument do you find more convincing? Cite examples from the articles as you explain your answer.

2. Charles Paul Freund and Neal Gabler agree that American television is losing its grasp on international audiences. Gabler, however, insists that American movies are still the standard-bearers of U.S. cultural imperialism. What do you think are the features of contemporary American films that foreign audiences enjoy? Do you think these elements indeed impose a type of imperialism? Consult articles outside this anthology to broaden and deepen the perspective of your answer.

3. Martha Bayles argues that many of America's popular culture exports are harming the country's reputation overseas. Instead of boosting positive American values, Bayles remarks that the majority of U.S. television, music, and movies are reflecting a nation that revels in violence, criminality, and coarse behavior. Do you agree with Bayles that American pop culture shows the world a civilization in decline? Or are there some benefits to spreading American pop culture? Why or why not?

Organizations to Contact

The editors have compiled the following list of organizations concerned with the issues debated in this book. The descriptions are derived from materials provided by the organizations. All have publications or information available for interested readers. The list was compiled on the date of publication of the present volume; the information provided here may change. Be aware that many organizations take several weeks or longer to respond to inquiries, so allow as much time as possible.

American Enterprise Institute (AEI)
1150 Seventeenth St. NW, Washington, DC   20036
(202) 862-5800 • fax: (202) 862-7177
Web site: www.aei.org

AEI is a nonpartisan organization dedicated to evaluating and dispensing information concerning U.S. government policy. The institute's main areas of research include economic policy, social and political studies, and defense and foreign policy. AEI publishes the bimonthly magazine *American Enterprise* and provides many of its publications on its Web site. It also sponsors globalization101.org, an online project providing information about the impact of globalization.

Carnegie Endowment for International Peace
1779 Massachusetts Ave. NW, Washington, DC   20036-2103
(202) 483-7600 • fax: (202) 483-1840
e-mail: info@carnegieendowment.org
Web site: www.carnegieendowment.org

The Carnegie Endowment for International Peace, a private, nonpartisan organization, encourages the United States to take an active role in international relations. The institution promotes foreign policy that encourages nations to work together and create global change. *Foreign Policy* magazine is the bimonthly publication of the Carnegie Endowment; other reports and publications can be found on its Web site.

Cato Institute
1000 Massachusetts Ave. NW, Washington, DC   20001-5403
(202) 842-0200 • fax: (202) 842-3490
Web site: www.cato.org

The Cato Institute is a libertarian research organization that bases much of its public-policy analysis on Jeffersonian philosophy. The institute promotes the spread of American political values and free-market systems, but questions the efficacy of military intervention abroad. The Cato Institute publishes *Cato Journal* three times a year, coinciding with the end of their tri-annual conferences. Other published materials covering all areas of public policy can be found on its Web site.

Center of Concern (COC)
1225 Otis St. NE, Washington, DC   20017
(202) 635-2757 • fax: (202) 832-9494
e-mail: coc@coc.org
Web site: www.coc.org

Basing much of its analysis of global issues on Catholic social teaching, the COC seeks to promote projects and initiatives that address global issues such as hunger, poverty, environmental protection, and social justice. The organization publishes fact sheets and reports on topics such as international economic and trade policies and poverty. Many of these are available on its Web site.

Global Exchange
2017 Mission St., #303, San Francisco, CA   94110
(415) 255-7296 • fax: (415) 255-7498
Web site: www.globalexchange.org

Global Exchange is a nonprofit human rights organization dedicated to increasing understanding of global issues within the United States and promoting solutions to these issues abroad. The institute examines the impact of both the U.S. government and American corporations worldwide. Many reports and publications on U.S. economic and military intervention are available on its Web site. Some of the recent issues covered include the war in Iraq, the U.S. role in the Israeli-Palestinian conflict, and general information on economic globalization.

The Heritage Foundation
214 Massachusetts Ave. NE, Washington, DC   20002-4999
(202) 546-4400 • fax: (202) 546-8328
e-mail: info@heritage.org
Web site: www.heritage.org

The Heritage Foundation provides research and information on current public policies from a conservative perspective. The foundation has supported recent administration initiatives such as the establishment of the Millennium Challenge Corporation, the deployment of troops to Iraq, and the refusal of financial aid for the Hamas-led Palestinian Authority. The Heritage Foundation Web site provides numerous online publications analyzing all areas of government policy.

The Middle East Policy Council (MEPC)
1730 M St. NW, Suite 512, Washington, DC   20036
(202) 296-6767 • fax: (202) 296-5791
e-mail: info@mepc.org
Web site: www.mepc.org

The MEPC works to inform and induce debate and discussion about U.S. government policies involving the Middle East. The organization publishes the quarterly journal *Middle East Policy*, which has covered issues such as the U.S. role in Iraq and the conflict between Israel and Palestine. The Web site offers links to other Web sites concerning the Middle East as well as suggested readings and other publications.

Millennium Challenge Corporation (MCC)
875 Fifteenth St. NW, Washington, DC   20005
(202) 521-3600
e-mail: web@mcc.gov
Web site: www.mca.gov

In 2004 the George W. Bush administration created the MCC to work in conjunction with the Millennium Challenge Account (MCA) as a new method for distributing economic aid to countries in need. The program awards aid to countries with governments that commit to sound economic policies, ruling justly, and investing in their citizens. The MCC's Web site provides updates on what countries are eligible for aid, what compacts have been signed guaranteeing funds to countries, and other developments taking place within the program.

The National Committee on United States–China Relations

71 W. Twenty-third St., Suite 1901
New York, NY   10010-4102
(212) 645-9677 • fax: (212) 645-1695
e-mail: info@ncuscr.org
Web site: www.ncuscr.org

The National Committee on United States–China Relations works to foster a greater understanding of the relationship between the United States and China. Through numerous outreach and exchange programs as well as conferences and public education, the organization encourages the continued development of healthy relations between the two countries. Most of its newsletters and reports are available on its Web site.

Peace Action

1100 Wayne Ave., Suite 1020, Silver Spring, MD   20910
(301) 565-4050 • fax: (301) 565-0850
Web site: www.peace-action.org

Peace Action is a grassroots organization that believes war is not a viable option for conflict resolution. The organizations SANE and The Nuclear Freeze merged to create Peace Action after supporting numerous disarmament treaties over the past fifty years. The group continues to lobby for a U.S. foreign policy that promotes a reduction in weapons of mass destruction and eschews preemptive war as a foreign policy tool.

United Nations Educational, Scientific and Cultural Organization (UNESCO)

2 United Nations Plaza, Room 900, New York, NY   10017
(212) 963-5995 • fax: (212) 963-8014
Web site: www.unesco.org

UNESCO provides information on diverse cultural and educational issues facing the world in order to foster a greater understanding and respect for varying societies. The organization works within the United Nations to reduce poverty and increase education and development. One of the main areas of the organization's focus is culture and the impact of globalization on indigenous cultures around the world. Publications from UNESCO concerning global culture issues include the quarterly *Museum International*, the bimonthly *World Heritage Review*, and the online journal *UNESCO Courier*.

Washington Institute for Near East Policy

1828 L St. NW, Suite 1050, Washington, DC   20036
(202) 452-0650 • fax: (202) 223-5364
Web site: www.washingtoninstitute.org

The Washington Institute for Near East Policy is an organization dedicated to providing nonpartisan information to assist lawmakers and politicians in creating effective policies concerning the Middle East. The institute encourages policies in which the United States plays an active role in the region, helping both Americans and Middle Easterners. Many articles on topics pertaining to the region are available on the group's Web site.

Bibliography of Books

Samir Amin
The Liberal Virus: Permanent War and the Americanization of the World. New York: Monthly Review, 2004.

William Blum
Rogue State: A Guide to the World's Only Superpower. Monroe, ME: Common Courage, 2000.

Lael Brainard et al.
The Other War: Global Poverty and the Millennium Challenge Account. Washington, DC: Brookings Institution, 2003.

Noam Chomsky
Hegemony or Survival: America's Quest for Global Dominance. New York: Metropolitan, 2003.

Amy Chua
World on Fire: How Exporting Free Market Democracy Breeds Ethnic Hatred and Global Instability. New York: Anchor, 2004.

Tyler Cowen
Creative Destruction. Princeton, NJ: Princeton University Press, 2002.

Lane Crothers
Globalization and American Popular Culture. Lanham, MD: Rowman & Littlefield, 2006.

Dinesh D'Souza
What's So Great About America. New York: Penguin, 2003.

Alfred E. Eckes Jr. and Thomas W. Zeiler
Globalization and the American Century. New York: Cambridge University Press, 2003.

Ted Fishman — *China Inc.: How the Rise of the Next Superpower Challenges America and the World*. New York: Scribner, 2005.

Francis Fukuyama — *America at the Crossroads: Democracy, Power, and the Neoconservative Legacy*. New Haven, CT: Yale University Press, 2006.

Richard Haass — *The Opportunity: America's Moment to Alter History's Course*. New York: Public Affairs, 2005.

Stanley Hoffmann — *Chaos and Violence: What Globalization, Failed States, and Terrorism Mean for U.S. Foreign Policy*. Lanham, MD: Rowman & Littlefield, 2006.

Robert Jervis — *American Foreign Policy in a New Era*. New York: Routledge, 2005.

James Kitfield — *War & Destiny: How the Bush Revolution in Foreign and Military Affairs Redefined American Power*. Washington, DC: Potomac, 2005.

Charles Kupchan — *The End of the American Era: U.S. Foreign Policy and the Geopolitics of the Twenty-first Century*. New York: Knopf, 2002.

Carol Lancaster and Ann Van Dusen — *Organizing U.S. Foreign Aid: Confronting the Challenges of the Twenty-first Century*. Washington, DC: Brookings Institution, 2005.

Alexander T.J. Lennon, ed. — *The Battle for Hearts and Minds: Using Soft Power to Undermine Terrorist Networks.* Cambridge, MA: MIT Press, 2003.

Robert J. Lieber — *The American Era: Power and Strategy for the 21st Century.* New York: Cambridge University Press, 2005.

William H. Marling — *How "American" Is Globalization?* Baltimore: Johns Hopkins University Press, 2006.

Joseph S. Nye — *The Paradox of American Power: Why the World's Only Superpower Can't Go It Alone.* New York: Oxford University Press, 2002.

George Packer — *The Assassins' Gate: America in Iraq.* New York: Farrar, Straus & Giroux, 2005.

Clyde Prestowitz — *Rogue Nation: American Unilateralism and the Failure of Good Intentions.* New York: Basic, 2003.

Christian Reus-Smit — *American Power and World Order.* Malden, MA: Polity, 2004.

Tom Segev — *Elvis in Jerusalem: Post-Zionism and the Americanization of Israel.* New York: Metropolitan, 2002.

Alexander Stephan, ed. — *The Americanization of Europe: Culture, Diplomacy, and Anti-Americanism After 1945.* New York: Berghahn, 2006.

Stephen M. Walt   *Taming American Power: The Global Response to U.S. Primacy.* New York: Norton, 2005.

Index